LETTERS FROM THE EN

Cover: Ralph Whitlock in 1992 overlooking his home village (photo by Roger Pearce)

ROGER PEARSE · 90

Letters from the English Countryside

A selection of articles from the Guardian Weekly

Ralph Whitlock
Illustrations by Roger Pearce

EX LIBRIS PRESS

First published in 1992 by
EX LIBRIS PRESS
1 The Shambles
Bradford on Avon
Wiltshire

Typeset in 11 point Century Schoolbook

Design and typesetting by Ex Libris Press

Cover printed by Shires Press, Trowbridge
Printed and bound in Great Britain by
Dotesios Ltd., Trowbridge, Wiltshire

ISBN 0 948578 50 5

CONTENTS

ACKNOWLEDGEMENT

May I express my best thanks to those of my correspondents whose letters have been quoted in this book and whose permission is assumed. Where would we be without you?

Ralph Whitlock

Happy Days – with no modern conveniences

February 18th, 1990

"IS seven your lucky number, Grand-dad?" I was asked, "February 7th was your birthday, and now you're seventy-seven."

That question and the snow that fell that day set me thinking about my arrival in this world on that night in 1914. Was it snowing then? I think not, or I would have heard about it. I have been told that my father had to get out of bed at two o'clock in the morning and cycle six miles over the hills to Salisbury to fetch the doctor, who had to dress, harness his pony and trap, and make the reverse journey to our village. The baby had safely arrived well before he did.

It was, I suppose, unusual to summon a doctor for such an ordinary event. Although no nurse lived in our village, most expectant mothers relied on neighbours who had had plenty of experience as midwives. However, the circumstances were rather special, for my parents, who had long wanted a family, had to wait thirteen years for the arrival of myself, their firstborn, and my mother was thirty-six. So I was important to them, though my importance tended to become a little diluted by the arrival of a brother and sister in the next few years.

What was it like, the world in which I found myself in that last glow of sunset before the nightmare of the First World War? Well, my father's expedition that February night helps to set the scene. No telephone to summon the doctor. No cars. No local doctor or nurse. Incidentally, the weather records for that time reveal that the winter was mild, with "few frosts in January and February and much rain", so perhaps my father had a wet journey.

I was born in one of the two bedrooms of our cottage on the terraced hillside of the valley in which our village sits. My father, who had started his working life as a shepherd, had recently acquired the tenancy of twelve acres of farmland and so at last, at the age of forty, had his foot on the first rung of the farming ladder. From our windows we could look out on a yard and some miscellaneous buildings in the process of being developed into a proper farmstead. A grey New Forest pony, named Gipsy, joined our household soon after I did and was stabled in a derelict cottage at the bottom of our access path.

As our family grew, my brother and I were settled in

the second of the two bedrooms where we spent the nights all through our school and adolescent years, though in the 1920s our father built a new wing to the cottage. That gave me an early lesson in the pattern of sunshine and shadows of life. Exciting and fascinating though the building of the new house was, the clearing of the site meant the sacrifice of the old apple tree in which the goldfinches nested and under which I could pick up lovely red Tom Putt "fallers" in autumn.

Life was by present-day standards primitive. My parents' bedroom was furnished with a commode, but we children made do with a chamber-pot under the bed. Our downstairs lavatory was in a shed adjoining the house – a visit involving only a few steps out-doors, which made us more fortunate than many of our neighbours who had to trudge the length of the garden to the privy, next to the pigsty. On cold winter nights, such as we have been experiencing recently, our bed was warmed by bricks, heated in the oven and wrapped in flannel.

In our kitchen cum living room downstairs we had a black kitchen range, reputed to be the first ever installed in our village. It fitted on the open hearth, from which you could peer up the chimney and see the sky. The massively thick wall to the right of the range held a bread-oven where my mother baked a batch of loaves most weeks. From the low, black-beamed ceiling was suspended a bacon rack which always held some sides of home-cured bacon and a ham or two.

On Saturday nights we children were bathed in a big galvanised-iron bath in front of the fire, and I suppose my parents did the same after we had been put to bed. Or perhaps they just "washed all over". Sometimes, when my brother and I were small, neighbours would come to the house for potatoes or eggs or something while we were in the bath. They were invited to stand inside the door while my mother served them and no-one was in the slightest embarrassed.

The kitchen was quite a large room, with a built-in dresser, a large table in the centre, a grand-father clock, a harmonium, a rocking chair for my mother and a wooden armchair for my father. The only other downstairs room was a long, narrow pantry, not much more than a corridor. Just inside the pantry door, perched on wooden stools, were large earthenware water-pans with board covers. These contained our drinking water, drawn fresh daily from a deep well by bucket and windlass, with a double supply on Saturday to last over the weekend.

We had no kitchen sink, washing-up being done in bowls on the big table. On Mondays the week's clothes-wash took place in a room in the derelict cottage down the path, next to the pony's stable. The water was heated in a copper on the otherwise disused hearth. Chopping up wood for the Monday wash was another Saturday job. At home the kitchen fire was never allowed to go out, except on Fridays, when my mother black-leaded the grate. We could not, of course, have even a cup of tea without first boiling the kettle on the stove.

My parents had had thirteen years to grow used to the domestic routine before their family arrived. They were Victorian, both by birth and upbringing, and conversation at mealtimes tended to be much about old times and old-timers, which probably has had much to do with my interest in such matters.

In retrospect it all sounds incredibly primitive and even deprived, but we didn't find it so, not having the amenities of the 1990s to compare it with. Almost all the homes in our village were much the same as ours, and I remember ours as a happy, busy, friendly place.

The Enigmatic Hare

February 10th, 1991

ON an afternoon in the middle of January I was really surprised to see a white stoat in our local wood, here in southern England. I suppose the number of similar experiences I have had would not reach double figures, though I have seen a good many more in glass cases in country houses. Within my lifetime the automatic reaction to the sight of a white stoat was a blast from a double-barrelled gun.

In our southern shires most stoats retain their brown coat throughout the winter, though sometimes they experience a partial change, producing a kind of piebald effect. What triggers off the change is not clear, but it occurs within the space of a few days. Obviously white has camouflage value in snow, and it may be significant that we had two or three days of snow in mid-December. A Scottish colleague to whom I was relating this incident commented, "Och aye, all our stoats turn white in winter," which is only a slight exaggeration. Then he added, "Our hares do, too," and that isn't correct.

In Britain we have two species of hare, namely, the Brown Hare and the Mountain or Blue Hare (the blue refers to a blue-grey tinge to the summer coat). The Brown Hare occurs thoughout England and in all except the northernmost counties of Scotland. The Mountain Hare is found in most of Scotland, all Ireland, and a few northern English counties. It is only the Mountain Hare which switches to a white coat in winter, involving a regular winter moult, though not normally in Ireland.

As it happens, I have several queries about hares, which accumulated when I was ill back in the autumn. One asks, "Is it true that hares can hear thunder long before we can?" I think it likely enough and that is no more than might be expected in view of the the hare's huge ears.

In fact, though, having kept hares as pets in my youth, I can testify that they all enjoyed thumping with their front paws or back legs on wooden or cardboard boxes – anything that would give a good echo. One of my boyhood friends at one time had three hares – an adult and two young. When the adult grew tired of playing with the youngsters she gave a warning stamp with her back feet. The youngsters fell motionless and remained so for some time.

Years ago I used to fly fairly frequently from London to Northern Ireland landing at Nutts Corner airfield, which then served Belfast. The airfield was alive with hares, assembled in great packs (these, of course, would be Mountain Hares). When in due course the airfield was moved to a new site four miles away I wondered whether the hares would move too. Sure enough they did. I can only conclude that the hares liked the noise of the aircraft, or perhaps the vibrations they caused in landing and taking off.

Another reader repeats the old belief that hares do not drink. Can I confirm it? No. I can accept that hares may be able to go for quite long periods without apparently drinking, if they are feeding on wet vegetation, but they are quite capable of drinking and therefore I think, they probably do so.

When discussing hare idiosyncracies the other evening I was surprised at some of the items of country lore that surfaced. Doe hares usually have two leverets at a birth, but apparently a widely held tradition says that when there are three the third one has a white star on its forehead, I cannot comment, though I have seen hares with white stars.

Does the mother hare give birth to her babies in different places (for each leveret is subsequently found occupying a solitary squat), or does she pick them up and carry them? It seems to be a common belief among countrymen that she carries them, grasping them by the scruff of the neck, as a cat does kittens, but I have never met anyone who has actually seen this.

Is the hare a ruminant animal? No, in spite of the fact that rural folk-lore insists that it chews the cud, quoting the Book of Leviticus as evidence. But there is a difference.

A cud-chewing animal regurgitates its food and gives it a second mastication at its leisure, hours after first swallowing it, whereas a hare allows the undigested food to pass through it and then eats its own pellets.

What about this story of horned hares? This was a yarn once widely believed, and I think we may have dealt with it before. Oliver Goldsmith, for instance, asserted that not only were there "hares that were entirely black but even some have been found with horns, though these but rarely". It is true that horned hares were once to be found in country house collections of animal trophies, but they owed their existence entirely to the skill of a taxidermist.

Any day now hares will start their display antics which have led to the saying "as mad as March hares." These boxing bouts may be either two jack hares scrapping or a female (a "jill") seeing off an unwelcome male – it's impossible to tell which. Recently I have seen reports that hares are suffering from an epidemic that threatens to decimate them, and during the past decade there has been some diminution in numbers.

But on the downland farms around my home they are as plentiful as ever – more so than they have recently. And long may they flourish.

Shot with a Silver Gun

February 18th, 1990

"AND what may you be up to now?" I enquired of a keeper whom I met constructing some sort of wire-netting cages in the woods. "These are traps for pheasants," he explained. "It's time to catch the hens now."

So he introduced me to a facet of pheasant lore which was new to me. After the shoots on Boxing Day and the New Year the birds are systematically trapped. The hens are taken away to breeding pens; the cocks, except for a minority of selected ones for breeding, are released. Most of the hens on an estate are rounded up in this way, and that is why most of the pheasants that fall to the guns in January shoots are cocks. Quite a scientific procedure, for the pheasant is polygamous; cocks in any numbers are superfluous.

The programme earlier this century, as I remember it, was somewhat different. The hen pheasants were allowed freedom to choose their nesting sites, but the efficient keeper knew where most of them were. When a full clutch of eggs had been laid he removed them to a breeding-pen near his home where they were hatched by domestic poultry. The keepers called on all the poultry-keeping farmers of the neighbourhood, buying any hens, or even more ideally bantams that had gone broody.

They paid a very good price, and also offered a reward to anyone who could show them a pheasant's or partridge's nest that they had missed. Farm workers could earn a useful bit of pocket-money by keeping their eyes open. But my father used to assure me that it was all very tame and respectable compared to what formerly went on.

So next time I met my long-deceased great-grandfather William down the orchard under the old apple-tree where he used to set up his cider-press, I innocently enquired what did go on. Great-grandfather was about coeval with the nineteenth century, having died in 1882 not far short of eighty years of age. So he was a young man through the grim old days of man-traps and spring-guns and when taking a pheasant earned seven years' transportation to Australia. Not that country chaps were in any way deterred. In times of near-famine, when agricultural wages were seven shillings a week, cock pheasants worth twelve-shillings-and-sixpence merited a few risks.

"Does, 'shot with a silver gun', mean anything to you?" enquired my great grandfather, a twinkle in his eye.

It didn't, so he explained how the law of supply and demand operated with pheasants.

Poaching for the pot was unusual, though a cottager spotting a fine pheasant in his back garden and having a hungry family indoors would doubtless find means of bringing the two together. In general, though, he worked to supply a known market.

In almost every village there was a depot, to which poached game could be taken. Sometimes it was the village smithy or a cellar in the inn, sometimes a barn or granary. From there horse-drawn vehicles with legitimate business would take a load of pheasants, partridges and hares, well concealed under sacks of hay or other merchandise to the nearest stage-coach posting station. There the contraband would be transferred to the stage-coach, again well concealed.

At the peak of the stage-coach era it is said that three hundred coaches a day trotted past Hyde Park Corner. It seems to have been widely known that in the weeks before Christmas most of them carried a greater weight in clandestine dead passengers than in living ones.

In London there was no lack of customers. A London dealer testified to a Select Parliamentary Committee that he did business with nineteen thousand suppliers of game, most of them unregistered. The ultimate destination consisted of hotels, colleges, clubs, and other establishments where game-preserving gentry expected to dine as well as at home, if not better.

The Duke of Wellington, an advocate for the retention of the man-trap and spring-gun, recognised the ambiguity of his attitude when he wrote: "The poulterers of London refuse to buy pheasants killed by the gun. They must have been snared in order to suit their customers! Very soon they will require that they should be all hen pheasants!"

At the pinnacle of the market was the Lord Mayor of London's banquet at the Mansion House, which required that birds served should contain no shot. In other words, they had to be poached!

As late as 1859-60 Mrs. Beeton, in her first cookery book which included more than forty recipes for game, commented: "There are innumerable Acts of Parliament inflicting penalties on persons who illegally kill game, and some of them are very severe; but they cannot be said to answer their end. Nor can it be expected that ever they will, whilst there are so many persons of great wealth who have not otherwise means of procuring game except by purchase, and *who will have it!*"

"That", said my great-grandfather, "explains the meaning of 'shot with a silver gun!' The pheasants were paid for in silver."

"Not that ordinary village chaps were the only ones engaged in the trade," he added. "The gamekeepers were at it, too. And where, as in our village, two big estates adjoined, we used to play one off against the other. Any pheasant eggs we found on one estate we used to sell the keepers on the other. They knew where they came from and would give us a better price for them!"

'Shooting with a silver gun' would seem to be an expression that might have a modern application.

Why bother to migrate?

24th March 1991

AT this very minute an estimated six billion (six thousand million) birds are winging their way northwards across Europe from their winter quarters in Africa. Any day now I hope to see the advance guard of the invasion. Before most of our chalk downs in Wiltshire were ploughed I used to see both stone curlews and wheatears by the middle of March. The stone curlews arrived already paired off and mated, and I have found their eggs before the end of the month. Now the surviving pairs are confined mostly to land occupied by the Army (an invaluable undisturbed haven for them), while any wheatears we see are only passage migrants, on their way to breeding grounds farther north. The sandpits, too, where the sand martins (another early migrant) used to nest have been demolished, so the first migrant I am likely to record is the chiffchaff, whose monotonous little song I generally hear about March 21st. On a few occasions I have seen, too, the first swallow before the end of March.

It's a hazardous journey these birds make. Those which winter south of the Sahara have a thousand miles of desert to cross before they even see the sea. The three hundred mile crossing of the Mediterranean can be wild and stormy at this time of the year. Then comes the distressing gauntlet of the sporting guns (and nets and bird lime) of Italy, Spain, France and Greece which take a fifteen per cent toll of them (nine hundred million birds).

Why do they do it? Why bother?

The generally accepted explanation is that it started in the last Ice Age. As the ice crept farther south each year the birds retreated in autumn to escape the harsh winters but came back to their familiar nesting-grounds for the summer. Short journeys at first but becoming ever longer with the advance of the ice. And there are notable advantages in spending the summer in high northern latitudes, for not only is insect life abundant but the long summer days give the birds the maximum time to collect it for feeding their young. Well, if, as we are told, the latest major glaciation in the northern hemisphere occurred about a hundred thousand years ago, the birds have all that time to develop their migratory instinct, so it is no wonder they continue to exercise it, despite the formidable obstacles.

Just recently, however, I have had a letter from a Canadian reader telling me of some birds that have broken the pattern.They are Canada geese, and the scene of their defection is the the town of London, in southern Ontario. He writes:

> In spring and autumn the wild Canada geese fly overhead in their thousands, and countless numbers of them rest for a time and feed on gravel pits near our home. In the town we have a park in which there is a small children's zoo, with farm animals. A few springs ago a pair of Canada geese, resting on their northward journey, moved in with the domestic geese and swans and raised a family. In the autumn we expected them to go south with the migrating flocks, but No, they stayed in the park, even when the domestic geese were shut away in a barn for the winter. Here we have hard winters with lots of snow, and we thought the pair had made a fatal mistake,

but they survived and flourished.

Not only that, but when the migrating flocks arrived from the south in the spring some of them stayed in the park with our pair and nested there. In a few short years our flock has grown to around six hundred! They are still wild and free but never leave town. They have become quite a feature of the place, putting on spectacular air displays for our benefit and honking loudly as they fly. They have, though, become quite a headache for the park-keeper. You can imagine what a mess six hundred geese make of his lawns, and more wild geese join them every year.....

Yes, I can imagine the mess, and sooner or later someone will have to tackle the problem.

This is a remarkable example of birds successfully jettisoning their migratory instinct, but it occurs to me that here in England we have a parallel instance, involving the same species. Canada geese were introduced to England three hundred or so years ago, as ornamental waterfowl for private parks. Probably the earliest ones were pinioned, so they wouldn't have been able to migrate, but now we have a resident population estimated at around twenty thousand which show no inclination to migrate. Their maximum journeys seem to be from their nesting-sites in parks and farms to local stubble-fields to feed on the scattered grains on moonlit nights after harvest.

Over the past few years, too, another bird has been showing some inclination to avoid the hazards of migration and winter in England. A few blackcaps, which normally migrate with other warblers, have long been recorded as wintering in Devon, but in recent years more and more of them have been staying in counties all across the south of England. The other morning one was sitting on the cotoneaster bush just outside my study window and peeping in at me as I sat typing!

Royal Fool

1st April 1990

DO you remember the particular vigilance we needed to display in our school-days on April 1st? "Hey! Your shoe-lace is undone!", "Look out! There's a spider just going to drop on your head!". "Yah! April Fool!"

And our joyous rejoinder when a schoolmate not fully conversant with the rules challenged us after twelve o'clock mid-day? "April Fool's gone past, And you're the bigger fool at last!"

They were, of course, mere shadowy survivals of the more full-blooded practical jokes in which our fathers and grandfathers used to engage. How many gormless apprentices were sent off to the village shop for a packet of hurdle-seed! Or to the shoemaker's for two-pennyworth of Leather-me-quick! Or to the Builder's for "some sky-hooks, to help support this scaffolding!" Or to buy "a rubber hammer!", which is a joke that has entirely lost its point, for you can indeed buy rubber hammers now.

Far more elaborate hoaxes were sometimes perpetrated and were calculated to leave everyone wondering. I myself got involved, inadvertently, in one a few years ago. Invited to take part in a country television programme on truffle-hunting, I gave a straightforward account of how and where the truffles were found, how the dogs were trained to find them and other relevant details.

By chance (or so the producer told me!) the programme was scheduled to go on the air around April 1st, so a new character was introduced – an actor who gave a lively and convincing account of truffle cultivation as it never was practised! The programme ended with a reminder of the date, and left it to the viewers to decide which was the true and which the false version. I gather a good many of them got it wrong!

Then there were the treacle mines! I used to hear about these, in connection with April lst, in my youth but never had any first-hand information about them until, only a few weeks ago, I received a letter from a Plymouth reader. She tells me that as recently as 1980 an old lady who lived in a northern suburb of Plymouth, when asked her address would always reply that she lived "at Whitleigh, up by the old treacle mines".

Nearby is a deep ravine through which flows the Budshead stream:

One day it was noticed that there was a brown sediment in the water, and all kinds of officials came to look at it. They feared sewage contamination but could find no broken drains, and people living nearby said there was no unpleasant smell.

This happened in 1981, and later that year subsidences made some huge holes in the neighbourhood. A search in the city's archives revealed maps which showed that these were the 'old treacle mines', and the staining of the water must have been due to seepage from them. So the mines were properly capped, and there has been no recurrence of the problem.

Much has subsequently been written about them. So far as is known, there are only two outcrops of theriaciferous rock in Britain from which treacle can be obtained .... at Dunchideock and Tamerton, both in Devon. The latter is considered the finer of the two by connoisseurs. It is known to experts as 'Royal 12' , because it needs to be allowed to mature for twelve years, as against ten years for the Dunchideock product....

The story of the discovery of the mines is linked with that of a Lady Tamerton, 'one of the most famous beauties of the court of Charles II'. One day when she was riding round her castle at Tamerton she was set upon by gypsies and was rescued by a passing miner, returning to his home in Cornwall. When she offered this Zachariah Rose a reward he asked for a mining concession on the estate. She agreed, on condition that she was to have a percentage of what he found.

It wasn't long before Zachariah found a stratum of theriaciferous rock. She used her influence to secure for him and his heirs forever the right to exploit the deposit. Again, she stipulated that she should be supplied for all time with the treacle, 'for she considered that it helped to maintain her famous peaches-and-cream complexion.' The King also wanted his share – small tub every Michaelmas, and this custom continued for centuries.

'Royal 12' was also exported to America, where it was employed as an ingredient of the celebrated Brooklyn Fudge. It was also exported to behind the Iron Curtain and was reputed to be relished as a delicacy in the Kremlin. The true flavour can be only appreciated if taken in the same way as by Devonshire folk – mixed with equal portions of cider or whisky. Or spread, with a warm, non-metallic knife, on a layer of Devonshire cream on bread.

Anyone thinking of prospecting for theriacferous rock can observe the clues provided by three creatures of the wild, namely, the Alaskan bear (no use in Britain!), the hive bee and the ant. The bee has a natural affinity for the rock, but when its pouches have been filled it is so heavy that it has difficulty in flying. So watch for low-flying bees. The ant, it must be a red one, carries small lumps of ore on its head. So you look for a procession of heavily-laden red ants.

Does this leave you wondering?

A butterfly fluttering by

14th April 1991

YOU can hardly reckon the Small Tortoiseshell fluttering against the closed church window in a vain attempt to get out as the first butterfly of spring. The temporary warmth of a Sunday morning when the heating apparatus is functioning is responsible for its premature awakening from the deep sleep of hibernation. "Shall we open the window and let it out?" someone asks. "No" I advise, thinking of the morning frost. "It's kinder to let it stay. Maybe it will go to sleep again."

The distinction of being the first butterfly of spring almost invariably belongs to the Brimstone. No creeping into cosy crevices in churches, garden sheds, garages or attics for this insect. It is an outdoor creature for its whole life. Its favourite hibernaculum is deep in the recesses of a cluster of ivy leaves, where the camouflage provided by the shape of its wings and their very pronounced veins make it almost invisible.

For a few days in early spring,winter is forced into a temporary retreat. A gentle breeze winnows through from the south, the sun beams down with unaccustomed warmth, and the daisies open their hearts to it as the temperature approaches the magic figure of seventy degrees Fahrenheit. The earth is suddenly alive again and vibrates with bird song, while the grass of lawns and meadows grow visibly. That is when on woodland walks we are startled to see newly-opened primroses apparently expand their petals and fly away.

They are, of course, Brimstone butterflies, which have a strong symbiotic relationship with primroses. The shape of the interior of a primrose flower and that of a Brimstone's tongue exactly coincide. Probably neither the butterfly nor the flower could flourish without the other.

Because the Brimstone is so closely associated with early spring (though later broods occur at other seasons, even into late autumn) it has evidently given its name to the whole race of butterflies. A brimstone is a fly the colour of butter – the derivation is as simple as that. Our ancestors who first gave names to the creatures of the countryside had a flash of inspiration here.

It was on a day in the middle of March that I saw the first Brimstones in the woods this year. Frosts had given way to gloomy, murky weather, with morning mists that lasted till mid-day, but on this day the unfamiliar sun stages a triumphant return, and on an hour's walk I saw no fewer than eight butterflies. Not all together, but one here and one there, scattered about the woodland rides, doubtless looking for primroses. Very strong on the wing are Brimstones, and they have need to be, for although they are so attracted by primroses (as well as by a whole range of summer flowers) their caterpillars feed exclusively on two rather uncommon bushes, the buckthorn and the alder buckthorn. The butterflies often have to fly for miles in search of these shrubs, the insignificant little flowers of which are of no interest to them.

An Australian reader who has been a photographer in his time sends me an intriguing account of another butterfly idiosyncracy. He writes:

> One of my clients wanted a colour transparency of a certain butterfly, which happens to be quite common,

so I caught one and popped it into the fridge for a few minutes. The effect of this procedure is to make the butterfly think it is night and so keep nice and still. I duly photographed it and then placed it on my finger in the sun, to warm up preparatory to flying away. When it had been vibrating its wings for a while and seemed ready to go, I tossed it into the air. It flew around in a circle of about six feet and landed back on my shoulder. This performance was repeated and repeated. I asked a lady who passed by, "How do you throw away a butterfly?" but she had no answer. Another more constructive citizen exclaimed, "Gee! how d'y' manage to teach it t'd THET?" Eventually I got someone else to hold it while I nipped inside my office. When he called, "OK to come out," it had gone."

The narrator tells me that at the time he was wearing a dark red shirt, which may have had something to do with the attraction, especially if the colour of the butterfly matched the shirt. That does not necessarily follow, however, for, in England, although our Brimstone is so attracted by the similarly-coloured primroses in spring, in high summer it seems to have a distinct preference for purple flowers, such as thistles, teasels and knapweeds.

....Hot Cross Buns

12th April 1987

A GRAND-DAUGHTER of mine, who has chosen to make a career of baking (of all things!), has been busily making hot-cross buns since the middle of February. "What are your doing – stock-piling them?" I enquired. "No, there's already a steady demand for them," she assured me.

When I was a boy such matters were left till Good Friday morning, when the village baker was up before three o'clock so that the old fellow with the handcart could deliver hot-cross buns in time for breakfast. I remember that old and decrepit delivery-man mumbling, as he trudged along the street, the traditional chant which we children knew well.

Hot Cross buns! Hot Cross buns!
One-a-penny, two-a-penny,
Hot Cross buns!
If you have no daughters, give them to your sons;
One-a-penny, two-a-penny,
Hot Cross buns!

I doubt whether I would now appreciate those curranty, cinnamon-flavoured buns for breakfast, but they tasted good then.

Although I don't remember ever putting the matter to the test, we were told that cakes or bread baked on Good Friday would last fresh all the year. It would never go mouldy and, when crumbled and powdered could be used for curing indigestion! Good Friday loaves were marked with a cross not only because of their religious associations but to prevent them from being eaten prematurely by mistake. If kept for a whole year they were moistened and eaten for tea on Easter Day.

Significantly, all the early spring festivals – Palm Sunday, Good Friday, Easter – have associations with food. No doubt this was because Easter marks the end of the austere season of Lent, when food of all kinds used to be in short supply at the end of winter.

On Palm Sunday it was the custom for the people of Avebury, in North Wiltshire, to march in procession to the top of Silbury Hill, that colossal and mysterious mound of earth that has archaeologists baffled, there to eat fig cakes and sugar water. In the same county the villagers of Maiden Bradley used to climb steep-sided Bidcombe Hill and sit around a grassy depression near the top, eating 'furmety', which apparently is a kind of wheaten porridge. The depression is still known as 'The Furmety Hole'. No doubt because of similar associations Palm Sunday used to be called Fig Pudding Day in the Cotswolds.

The special sweetmeat for Easter Day was Easter cakes which were flat, biscuit-like, scalloped-edged confections, studded with currants and sprinkled with sugar. I believe they can still be bought, but ours were home-made.

Great-grandmother Elizabeth used to make hers with wafer irons, which were long tongs with two flat plates at the end. She had her own recipe, which has now been lost. As she lived next door to the blacksmith she used to take the tongs and the batter down to the smithy, get the smith to make the tongs very hot in the forge fire, and then squeeze the mixture tight between two plates.

She used to colour the cakes or biscuits bright yellow with meadow saffron, of which a thriving colony of plants existed in a meadow down the lane. Unfortunately, by order of the War Agricultural Committee, the meadow was ploughed up during the 1939/45 war.

Hot Cross buns, Good Friday bread and wafer biscuits were all valued apart from their culinary attractions. Stored in an airtight tin and hung up over the hearth, they were reckoned a good luck talisman and also a protection against the house catching fire.

When at one time in the Scottish Highlands at this season, I was told that the Good Friday traditions there tended to be associated with Maunday Thursday, which is also St. Columba's Day. A flat loaf or bannock was made on the previous day and baked over a wood fire. One tradition said the fire had to be of one or more of the sacred trees – rowan, oak or yew. On Maunday Thursday the bannock was cut into several pieces, according to the number of children in the household, and the child who found a coin in its slice was duly rewarded.

The associations of Good Friday are also with the growing of food as well as the eating of it. Good Friday is the 'day ordained for the planting of taties', according to the reply, now become almost proverbial, alleged to have been given by a devoted gardener to a parson.

As potatoes have been commonly grown in Britain for less than two centuries the tradition would seem to be fairly recent, but perhaps it was adapted from something similar but much older. A thought about mediaeval practice, whereby saints' days were holidays but Saturdays were not, helps us to appreciate that Good Friday did offer a providential opportunity for sowing garden seeds.

It puzzles me, though, to reconcile this with the widespread belief, which has been discussed earlier in this column, that seeds in general must be sown when the moon is waxing. As Easter Sunday is the first Sunday after the first full moon after March 20th, Good Friday is bound to coincide with a waning moon. Perhaps potatoes are considered an exception to the general rule, like peas and beans which, for some unfathomed reason, must be sown when the moon is waning.

Rock-a-bye Dormouse

21st June 1988

IT was a surprise to find a dormouse's nest some four or five feet from the top of a thirty feet conifer which had just come crashing to the ground. The nest was occupied, too, by a sleepy dormouse which took twenty minutes to wake up. The inference was that it was still hibernating, although by that date (May 4th) I would have expected it to have been up and about.

Although a tree-top hibernaculum is unusual, dormice are more arboreal than is sometimes supposed. In the days when cottagers often kept them as pets, their familiarity was due to the fact that country workmen frequently disturbed them dormant in their winter nests in the hedgerows. So the legend grew that they were creatures of hedges and shrubby coppices, whereas their active life is spent mainly in tree tops.

One of the current tasks of our local forest park is to widen the rides to admit more sunlight and air. Already it is producing encouraging results in the greater profusion of woodland flowers and butterflies. But the other day a visiting naturalist who has studied dormice offered a warning. Dormice, he said, will never descend from the tree-tops to cross a ride. They circulate entirely in the tree canopy, moving from tree to tree by way of intertwining branches. So when widening rides and tracks we should leave corridors of overhanging trees as access between the several sectors of woodland. This is good advice which we shall, of course, take, but it is a point which would not have occurred to us. After all, grey squirrels, which are also arboreal and which are related to dormice, travel freely along the ground.

Doubt exists as to the real status of dormice nowadays. Are they really so much scarcer than they used to be be or are they less frequently seen simply because the woodland workers and manual hedge-cutters have almost vanished? I am inclined towards the second theory, for dormice seem to be fairly well distributed in our woods. Boys from a local centre for the mentally handicapped make batches of nest-boxes (mostly for tits) for us each year. Last year we had about a hundred and fifty in position, of which about seventy per cent – a gratifying ratio – were occupied. But when we checked them in late autumn we discovered that several were being used a second time. They contained snug nests, filling the entire box and evidently occupied, presumably by dormice. We left them to sleep in peace.

One sunny day last spring I did encounter a bit of confirmatory evidence. I lifted the lid of a tit nest-box, and a dormouse popped out and ran up my arm. It duplicated an experience I had as a boy, when I found a long-tailed tit's nest in a honeysuckle thicket. Several days later I revisited it and unwisely inserted a finger to discover how many eggs had been laid. A dormouse pushed past my finger and dropped to the ground. But I had disturbed it at a meal; nearly all the eggs had been sucked!

Specialists who have studied the animals say that eighty per cent of dormice fall prey to predators during hibernation, but that is not surprising, for most of them seem to spend about eighty per cent of their time asleep. In their relatively brief period of activity they are nocturnal so are not the easiest of animals to observe, but cottagers who have kept them as pets have told me that when they wake up in the evenings they are exceedingly lively and active. In the wild they appreciate the presence of sweet chestnut, brambles, wayfaring tree and, of course, hazel and honeysuckle. From the honeysuckle they strip off bark to make their nests, and the hazel supplies them not only with nuts but with pollen from the catkins, a protein-rich food much appreciated by individuals who wake up briefly in early spring.

The dormice which the Romans used to fatten and eat were not our English species but the edible or fat dormouse (scientific name – *Glis*), which is only a little smaller than the grey squirrel. Some were brought over from the Continent early this century and released at sites in the Chilterns, where they still flourish, as I discovered a few years ago when I asked to investigate mysterious noises emanating from the rafters of a woodland residence. Bumps, scratching, shuffling, squeaking, scampering were all graphically described to me; the people thought they had a poltergeist. Realising, however, that I was in the right part of Hertfordshire I had little difficulty in identifying the culprits, though how to banish them was another matter. Once edible dormice have taken up residence they are extraordinarily difficult to dislodge. However, all was well, for the family was quickly reconciled to living with their lodgers, now that they knew what they were.

It might have been expected that the edible dormouse,

finding itself in an eldorado of beeches, would quickly spread over the countryside of southern England, but it proves to be no great traveller. Once established, it is content with an almost sedentary life, seldom moving more than a quarter-of-a-mile from base. And that is all to the good, for the edible dormouse is no friend to foresters, being addicted to gnawing the bark of timber trees in order to get at the sapwood.

Incidentally, I continue to receive letters about magpies, most of them as disapproving as that from a reader in Saskatoon who describes them as "urban vultures" and can find nothing good to say about them. Let me provide him with further ammunition – they eat dormice!

A-primrosing down Cock-road

3rd April 1988

ALTHOUGH 'down memory's lane' may seem a somewhat trite expression, it describes exactly a nostalgic little pilgrimage I indulged in the other day. With about an hour to spare before picking up my wife from a visit she was making in the village where we were both born, I decided to take a look at the site of the old cottage at the bottom of Dunley Hill. Probably owing to the mild winter, 1988 is proving to be a remarkable year for snowdrops. They are flaunting themselves in profusion everywhere, and I wondered whether those which had once adorned that cottage garden had survived.

They had. The cottage itself, a cob-and-thatch building, was disintegrating when I was a boy, though my father could remember when it was occupied. On Sunday afternoons, disregarding the admonitions of our parents, we boys used to clamber about the ruins, sometimes venturing up the rickety stairs to slide down the steeply slanting bedroom floor. But that was a fleeting memory, for chalk cob speedily dissolves when it loses its hat. Now even the foundations are no longer visible, and the garden is lost in bushes and brambles.

However, the old yew tree, under which Elijah Collins' outdoor privy used to stand, has apparently aged not at all. And the snowdrops have done more than hold their own; some are blooming now on the very site of the cottage.

To get here I strolled along the half-mile or so of

Slateway, an undistinguished lane having as its chief function access to the local big estate. Why 'Slateway'? I asked when I started to take an interest in local etymology, and was even more intrigued when I found that an older name was 'Slay-gate Way'. It conjured up scenes of battle or at least poaching. I wondered who had been slain.

Alas, the name had nothing to do with violence and bloodshed. It was simply a corruption of 'Sloe-gate' – the place where sloes grow abundantly. And there, just as when I was a boy, is the same extensive thicket of blackthorn bushes, which bear the sloes.

'Dunley Hill' is more promising. The authorities on the subject say that the name derives from 'Daneley'– 'Danes' Meadow'. Well, here we are in the home territory of King Alfred, and the Danes against whom he fought so valiantly were undoubtedly here eleven hundred years ago. Eleven hundred years? As Dunley carves its tortuous way up the steep scarp it becomes a sunken way flanked by cliffs that are in places twenty feet deep. Would the frequent passage of human feet, horses' hooves and rustic vehicles cut a channel that deep in eleven hundred years?

On the summit of the hill Dunley merges with another lane, known as Cock-road. The name is said to indicate a place where in medieval times nets were spread for woodcock. As the fields which now flank it were carved out of hazel and oak woodland, that derivation is likely enough. Woodcock are still found hereabouts, wherever a sufficient area of woodland survives.

Cock-road now leads almost nowhere, though a few tractor tracks show that it is occasionally used by farm vehicles, and the now ubiquitous riding horses have discovered it. At one time it was a short cut between two villages, but the refusal of the County Council to be responsible for its upkeep, back in the 1920s, relegated it to the status of a green lane. In those days, when Sunday afternoon walks were a standard occupation for village folk, Cock-road was the equivalent of a stroll in the park for our village families.

It was so long ago that I last walked there that some of the things I saw combined half-submerged memories with the freshness of novelty. Back in 1920 the underwood industry was sufficiently flourishing for all the hazel still to be coppiced. A crop of sturdy hazel rods was cut every seven or eight years, and the adjacent bramble and weedy undergrowth cleared at every cutting. I remember seeing piles of wattle hurdles, bundles of spar-gads and great dumps of faggots, bean-rod and pea-sticks stacked alongside the lane. But what I had failed to notice or remember was that all the taller trees – the maples, oaks, ashes, and beeches – also bore evidence of once having been coppiced, their present trunks originating in young shoots sent up by decapitated stubs.

The margins of Cock-road now are more overgrown and

tangled than they were. The primroses, wood anemones, orchids and violets have a hard time competing with the rank vegetation which the underwood worker with his bill-hook used to keep regularly in check.

I walked as far as the great beech tree, on the edge of Hunt's Copse, the landmark at which our Sunday afternoon walks often terminated. Around it are dimly discernible outlines, in the form of flint foundations, of former buildings. Records from the time of the first Queen Elizabeth reveal that here stood the house, lodge and 'nut-store' of Henry Hunt, warden or keeper of this corner of the great estate. I expected to find the initials which we boys had cut into the bark of the tree, but time had obliterated them all. A new generation had marked on it their love messages in less durable chalk.

I have a special reason for retracing my steps down Cock-road at this reason. My father was a busy man. As a small farmer he milked his own cows, sowed his own corn, lambed his own flock of sheep, killed his own pigs and ran a market garden round, but he was also chairman of the parish council, Sunday School superintendent and deeply involved in all local affairs. I was therefore surprised when, one Good Friday when we were small, he announced that he was going to drop everything for the afternoon and come a-primrosing down Cock-road with the rest of us. My mother, my aunt, my brother and sister, and four or five neighbourhood children. We scampered about around the hazels, picking primroses and sweet violets, listening to the thrushes singing, looking for an early nest, watching the little black spiders rustling over the carpet of dead leaves.

My father lived a full and active life, with many achievements to his credit, but that is how I remember him most vividly, picking primroses with the family down Cock-road on a Good Friday afternoon.

Getting Together

9th February 1992

BY Valentine's Day birds have chosen their mates for the coming year. This is a common belief, and, although there is no scientific evidence, it is likely enough to be correct, for it is generally accepted that birds' nesting boxes ought to be in position by the middle of Februay. By then the days are noticeably longer and the birds' thoughts turn towards the nesting-season.

And not only the birds are affected. Valentine's Day is the traditional date for choosing one's partner. It is in fact directly developed from the Roman feast of Lupercalia, February 14th, when partners were chosen for the coming year by drawing lots. St. Valentine was a saint whose feast day happened to fall on the right date, and scandalised early Christian bishops tried to suppress the ancient custom, with only limited success.

As a matter of fact, the practice of sending Valentine cards antedates by a long time that of sending Christmas cards, which only became popular in Victorian times. A book of 1832 describes how, in Hertfordshire, the children of the parish assemble at 'the house of the chief personage of the place, who throws them wreaths and true lovers' knots from the window with which they adorn themselves. Two or three of the girls then select one of the youngest amongst them (generally a boy), whom they deck out more gaily than the rest and, placing him at their head, march forward in the greatest state imaginable, singing,

Good morrow to you, Valentine,
Curl your locks as I do mine,
Two before and three behind,
Good morrow to you, Valentine.

This they repeat under the windows of all the houses they pass, and the inhabitants seldom refuse. One woman is still remembered for having kept some of her best Blenheims for 'the singing boys and girls'.

Way back in the seventeenth century Samuel Pepys recorded in his diary, "I find that Mrs. Pierce's little girl is my Valentine, she having drawn me, which I was not sorry for, it easing me of something more than I must have given to others."

"They begin as early as six o'clock in the morning" says the Hertfordshire book quoted above, and in Norfolk it was held that if any child could say, "Good morrow, Valentine", twice before sunrise and before being spoken to he could demand a present.

A feature of the Feast of Lupercalis was the drawing of lots for partners for the coming year, and this lingered on till at least Victorian times. Young people of both sexes wrote their names on slips of paper dipped in clay and dropped into a bowl of water, to see the order in which they rose to the surface. Later, the first person of the opposite sex encountered on Valentine's Day was considered to be one's Valentine. But as the old customs died away so Valentine cards became more and more elaborate, and some of the Victorian ones were works of art. "The Valentine was a cushion of white satin or silk filled with delicately perfumed material. Around the edges was an elaborate design of embroidered paper, and at frequent intervals silver Cupids, with bows and arrows, silver pierced hearts, doves billing and cooing, orange blossom, lilies of the valley, roses and true lovers' knots."

Now there is a revival in the sending of Valentine cards, fostered entirely by the vendors of cards. Girls no longer pin bay leaves to the corners and centre of their pillows before going to sleep, in the hope of dreaming of their true love. Or wear their stockings inside out, to ensure getting a husband before the harvest moon rose. Or hang in the kitchen a bunch of early spring flowers tied with blue ribbon, transferring it to their bed at night. But the traditional belief still lingers, summed up neatly by an Exmoor couplet:

This is the day birds choose their mate.
And I choose you, if I'm not too late.

And the practical element is not forgotten, as exemplified by the rhyme:

By Valentine's Day
Every hen, duck and goose should lay.

Our ancestors used to thrash any hens that were not laying by Valentine's Day!

A pleasant letter from a reader in The Gambia, on reading what I wrote about stone curlew on December 8th. He writes:

> Along the side of the cut that we came through is a muddy ledge, mottled and pitted with holes like a Swiss cheese. Behind it is a mass of silvery reeds waving in the breeze, with the gleam of the green rice fields beyond. And on the ledge rest the Senegal Thick-knees, looking so like the stone-curlew depicted in your article. They are there in considerable numbers.

I think I know that ledge. It is by a stretch of the river known by the insalubrious name of Stink Corner, for obvious reasons, but ideal for all the wading birds on the river. The Senegal Thick-knee is very similar to our English stone-curlew, and I wonder whether some of the birds may not be ours. If so, they will soon be leaving for our fields, for they arrive in mid-march, already paired and eager to start nesting. They are almost the first spring migrant to arrive. And I misled you if I led you to believe that they had entirely abandoned us. There were twenty or thirty pairs nesting in Wiltshire last year, most on land occupied by the Army.

Start of the Lambing

2nd February 1992

I REMEMBER Candlemas Day (February 2nd) because that is the date by which the days are supposed to have lengthened sufficiently for us to have tea without artificial light! Mind you, the date sticks in my mind because it happens almost to coincide with my birthday, but, anyway, it marks one of the first signs that winter is passing away. And the first snowdrops are supposed to bloom on that day.

When I was a boy, too, that week was the occasion of hectic activity, preparing for the lambing. On our farm we had a Hampshire Down flock which started lambing in the first week of February. It seemed a crazy arrangement, lambing in the coldest month of the year, but actually it was based on the soundest calculations. Lambs dropped in February were ready to graze on the early spring grass at the end of March and were fat and ready for the butcher at the end of June, when the price of home-produced lamb was at its highest.

So in a sheltered field corner we prepared a lambing pen of wattle hurdles reinforced with straw. Along one side were individual lambing-pens, roofed over with straw and each just large enough to take a ewe and newborn lamb, as snug as could be.

In the first week of February the final touches were made and the shepherd took up residence in his mobile hut, a box on wheels with a galvanised iron roof, which would be his home for the next six weeks. His duty was to get up three or four times in the course of the night and do the rounds, transferring any newborn lambs and their mothers to the individual coops and seeing that they sucked. With twins he took the lambs into his hut and warmed them by his stove, which was always kept burning.

For those six weeks he only paid brief visits to his home, for a change of clothes and maybe a hot meal, but during those six weeks he ruled the farm. There being little else to do in the middle of winter, his needs were dominant. Every day there was a procession of carts and wagons from the farmyard to the lambing-pen, bearing hay and cake for the sheep and provisions for the shepherd. The farmer himself made the journey at least once a day. And if snow intervened the whole staff was kept busy clearing a track to the lambing-pen.

My great-uncle was a head shepherd, and he revelled in his importance. For six weeks he gave up his sleep and hot meals and cosy bed for the sake of the sheep, and he took good care that he was properly appreciated. I had the feeling that the broken nights and constant attention demanded by the flock were, in his opinion, a worthwhile price to pay for the position of paramount importance they secured for him. Besides which, he was paid a substantial bonus for the number of lambs reared above the number of ewes kept; in other words, a bonus on twins and triplets.

Nowadays most flocks lamb down in April, when they can lamb out of doors, though some stick to the traditional February date. The shepherd's hut, though, is a thing of the past. Those farms which go in for early lambing are well equipped with permanent buildings to house the lambing pens.

Folklore has been busy with Candlemas Day. A wet morning foretold a fine spring but if it was a bright, sunny day there would be snow before May Day – a fairly foolproof forecast, I would have thought.

But Candlemas omens are filled with warning:

In the barn on Candlemas Day
Should be half the straw and half the hay

In other words, winter is only half over. Half the winter livestock rations and half the household's supply of fuel should be still untouched. For:

As the day lengthens
So the cold strengthens

Better to put one's faith in the saying, 'A late spring never deceives'.

Candlemas, however, has a much more powerful hold on the imagination in America than in Britain. For in parts of the States it is celebrated as Groundhog Day, the groundhog being the woodchuck or prairie marmot. The theory is that the groundhog, which is a light hibernator, wakes up on this day and looks out of his burrow. If he sees his shadow there will be six more weeks of winter, but if the day is cloudy he will not return to his winter quarters, for spring is only just around the corner.

The occasion is celebrated with almost unbelievable ceremony. In Quarryville, Pennsylvania, for instance, members of the Slumbering Groundhog Lodge assemble in the early morning, suitably clad in nightshirts, top hats, and with golden keys suspended round their necks, and go out into the country to find the burrow of a groundhog. After disturbing the animal they wait for him to emerge from his burrow and pronounce on whether he has or has not seen his shadow. The Lodge claims one hundred per cent accuracy for the forecast, though official figures say they are correct only twenty-eight per cent of the time.

However, that does not prevent the members from engaging in fun and games. At a Wisconsin celebration they partake of a traditional breakfast consisting of moose milk, coffee, and sweet rolls. Other communities celebrate with dancing to the music of drums, guitars, fiddles, and piano. And at one of the oldest of such clubs, that of Punxsutawney, Pennsylvania, they serve an exotic menu featuring such delicacies as Woodchuck Jello Salad, Soothsayer Gravy, Steak a la Seer of Seers, and Forecaster Green Beans, with other accessories to match!

A Place in the Country

4th September 1988

"CAN I make you an offer for that old barn, Mr. Fairenough?"

"Now what would 'ee be wantin' that for?"

"Well, to be quite candid with you, I'm thinking of retiring down here, and I can see possibilities of making a period house of that barn. I'm prepared to spend a bit on it, so that it will still fit in with its surroundings."

"No, wouldn't think of it! I were left this cottage and the barn and they old sheds by my grandfather; and they belonged to his father and grandfather before en. Sort of a family heritage, see. Wouldn't dream of partin' wi' none of it."

"Well, if you change your mind..."

* * *

"I hear old Henry Fairenough has got planning permission for four houses alongside his place."

"Four?!"

"Yes. In a row. Low-cost ones, they're supposed to be, but he got top price for the sites. Going to pull down the old barn to make room for 'em."

"Crafty old devil! And I offered him a good price for that barn."

"Not as much as he got for the sites, though!"

* * *

"Why couldn't you have let me have that barn when I asked you, Henry? The conversion I had in mind would have matched the village better than a row of two-bedroomed units."

"Ah, but see, Mr. Innocent, I wur thinkin' of the village school."

"The village school?!"

"Aye. These young village people that wants to get married can' find nowhere to live, that they can afford. So they got to move off to the town. And that means no children in the village, and the school will have to shut down. We wouldn't want that to happen, now would we? We must look after our young people."

* * *

Three years later.

"I hear your Chris and Emma are moving out of their little house along Pond Lane. Where Henry Fairenough's old barn used to stand."

"Yes, they say they want a bigger place now the twins are becoming active. They're going into town. Still, they're making a good profit out of the house."

"Any idea who's coming in their place?"

"Yes, old Mr. and Mrs. Lately, from Wellhouse."

"They've got a nice house already."

"Ah, but it's too big for them now they've retired."

"That makes three of those four cottages are now occupied by retired couples. And they were supposed to be for young married people with children."

"Yes, but it didn't work out that way, did it?"

* * *

"Hullo, Henry. I hear you're moving out."

"Aye. Thought I would. Nothing much to keep I here

now."

"I thought you'd never part with your heritage, as your used to call it?"

"Ah, but times change. I 'llow I'll be a sight more comfortable in this bungalow I'm buying in town. All electric. Shan't be doin' any more work."

"Who's going to be our new neighbours?"

"Feller from Wimbledon or somewhere. Name of Milton."

* * *

"Good morning, Mr. Milton. Settling in all right?"

"So-so. By degrees. Bit difficult to get things done in the country now, though, it seems. Do you know, I can't get anybody to do a bit of gardening for me, for love nor money! Anyone would think you could get a jobbing gardener in a village like this. Isn't there anyone?"

"Well, there used to be. Old Henry Fairenough. But that's his house you've bought!"

* * *

All this worries me at times, so when next I met my great-grandfather William down the orchard, under the old apple-tree where his cider-press used to stand, I disburdened my soul to him.

"It seems to me all wrong," I said. "I was brought up to understand that you *earned* a living, by hard work or good business management. Nobody thought of making money by buying and selling their homes. The value of a house was much the same when you celebrated your golden wedding as when you got married and moved into it, now wasn't it? The general idea now seems to be to buy a cottage, effect a few improvements, make a fast buck by selling it and then move on. The only householders who stay put are the old people."

"Like old Henry Fairenough, I suppose?" he grinned maliciously. "No, you're only partly right. Some people made money out of buying and selling property much as they do now. I remember when farming was prosperous the old Earl of Itany split off great sections of his estate and sold them as small farms. Later, when the agricultural depression set in and farmers began to go bankrupt, he bought them back, dirt cheap."

"The only difference I can see," he went on, "is that in those days only the aristocrats, the landed gentry, could make money that way. Now, from what you've been telling me, everybody seems to be doing it!"

Hard Cheese – it's all downhill

21st April 1991

WERE the 'cheeses' used in the old-time summer sport of rolling cheeses down a hillside real cheeses or the skittles missile, often known at that time as a 'cheese'? My brief comment, of a few weeks ago, of a doubt on the matter has prompted a lot of correspondence, including a letter with the sensible suggestion, why don't you ask great-grandfather William? So the next time I met him down the orchard, under the rugged old apple-tree where he used to set up his cider press I did.

"Aye, we used to play skittles out-of-doors on summer evenings," William told me. "We used to set up the pins at the foot of Nadderbourne Hill, where it levels off into Parsons' meadow. Then we'd stand at the top of the hill and roll the cheese down the slope."

"So it was a skittles cheese – wooden one?".

"Oh, aye. I suppose it was called that because it was shaped just like a cheese. It was usually a section cut off a tree trunk – oak or elm as a rule – and heavy! My goodness, you had a job to lift some of they cheeses! That's why we trolled 'em downhill. Some of 'em were too heavy to lift; you just set 'em in the right position and pushed 'em."

"Mind you," he went on, "I have heard that up in north Wilts they did use real cheeses sometimes. But that's cheese country. You knows that?"

Yes, it's fairly widespread knowledge in the West

Country, though perhaps not elsewhere, that the expression 'as different as chalk from cheese' originated in Wiltshire. The southern two-thirds of the shire consists of chalk downland, with big arable farms grazed by sheep, whereas the north-western districts are clay meadows, occupied by smallholders with small dairy herds and therefore cheese-makers. Knowledgeable Wiltshiremen add 'and chalk is church and cheese is chapel' – a comment on the sectarian tendencies of the people, which is also true, or used to be.

"Some of they Wiltshire cheeses, you would certainly have had to push they downhill. I've seed some of they, at Weyhill Fair, that must have weighed nearer two hundredweight than one. It used to take two men to lift one – on a truckle – a kind of sledge contraption that you carried as though it were a stretcher. They used to tell me, when I were a boy that witches borrowed 'em to fly about the sky on 'em, of nights."

The practice of using real cheeses was therefore known and may have been widespread, for in Gloucestershire, where they have some superb slopes for the sport, several villages have a tradition of using Double Gloucester cheeses.

In case that should seem a waste of a splendid cheese. I have been told that when, as often happened, the cheese burst into pieces at the foot of the hill, the fragments were eagerly scrambled for by the spectators.

That would apparently never have happened with Wiltshire cheeses, which were so notoriously hard that they would have survived a worse battering than that intact. It was said that when a Wiltshire ploughman, at work in a field, noticed that his plough (a wooden one) needed tightening up he would cut a wedge from the cheese in his dinner bag and hammer it in!

Weyhill Fair, in the Hampshire village of Weyhill, near Andover, which was founded in the eleventh century, was at its most prosperous in great-grandfather William's time.

"We used to buy enough cheese there to last us the whole year," he remembered. "So did the hop growers who brought their hops over from Farnham. They used to arrive with their waggons loaded with hops and go home with them loaded with cheese."

William also recalled visiting relations on a cheese-making farm in north Wiltshire. "My uncle or cousin or whatever he was used to make about five tons of cheese a year, though some of the farms made a lot more than that. The cows they kept were what you would call Longhorns though of course they weren't pure-bred. A good cow would yield about four hundredweight of cheese a year. They used to reckon that their district was so well suited to cheese because each farm sat in the middle of its meadows, so the cows came in to be milked, instead of a milkmaid having to go with her stool and bucket to a distant field. As it was, all the milk was mixed at an even temperature.

"The cheeses they made were called Wilshire Loaves;

I don't suppose there are any of those about now?" (No, there aren't.) "There were the ordinary Loaves, and Flat Wiltshires and a Little Wiltshire, which was a soft little cheese, which you ate straight away, just out of the dairy.

"I remember my auntie was also experimenting with a blue veined cheese. She did that by crumbling up some mouldy bread, till it was blue with mould, and mixing that with the cheese while it was making."

That sounds to me something like Dorset Blue Vinny....But more of that another day.

Salesmanship in the Corn Market

10th October 1991

SOME little time ago I found myself sorting through the lumber in an old loft. There was little of interest in the junk – broken parts of machinery, tools so obsolete that their very use is forgotten, bits of old harness, part empty bags containing unidentifiable substances. I was intrigued to unearth an old chaff shovel, with a broad, wooden blade, once an indispensable feature of every stable but now having lain idle for the best part of a hundred years. It was of a type once made at Penton Mewsey, near Andover, at an establishment which was closed down over a century ago.

Then, in a corner under an accumulation of rubbish, I came upon an old cardboard folder, the use for which baffled me. It measured approximately eight inches by four and was folded twice, leaving a sort of pocket. Obviously it once contained something but I was uncertain what.

So the next time I met my great-grandfather William, down the orchard under the old apple-tree where he used to set up his cider press, I asked him if he could recognise it. He examined it, turning it this way and that and then, with a broad grin, said, "Yes, it's a sample pocket!"

Seeing my look of puzzlement, he proceeded, "It used to be the custom to take samples of grain to market in one of these. They were made to a certain pattern, and the whole of the inside of the folder was coloured a darkish blue. It was astonishing how much better the grain looked against a dark background. Certainly that was so with wheat and barley; the barley looked a steely blue and it fetched a better price than when shown in the open hand.

A farmer who knew what he was doing always wore a blue suit when he took samples to market, too, and he contrived to stand with his back to the light. Anyone who didn't know the tricks of the trade allowed himself to be manoeuvred into facing a north light, which showed up the defects!"

"A trick?" he countered, in response to a comment from me, "No, we called it 'salesmanship!'"

Mind you, the practice of selling grain by sample was a comparatively recent innovation. Just before great-grandfather William's time a writer refers to the universal custom of selling in a pitched market where grain was sold by the wagon-load. He quotes Salisbury, Devizes and Warminster as being outstanding examples of pitched markets, with Warminster predominant, and mentioned that as many as two thousand quarters (four thousand sacks) of wheat were sold there weekly. My father just remembered the corn market at Warminster and the teams of horses struggling to haul the great, heavily-laden wagons up the steep incline by the church, often axle-deep in mud.

Although the practice ceased soon afterwards it died hard, as farmers used to like striking a bargain and receiving payment in cash the same day. "Generally before three o'clock," says one comment, thus allowing plenty of time to get home before dark – an important consideration before the days of banknotes and cheques, when large sums had to be carried in the form of guineas.

A hazard likely to be encountered is illustrated by a memorial stone, often hidden by long grass, that stands at the junction of the Devizes highway with the by-road

to the abandoned village of Imber. The interesting inscription records that:

> At this spot Mr. Dean of Imber was attacked and robbed by four highwaymen in the evening of October 21st 1839. After a spirited pursuit of three hours one of the felons, Benjamin Colclough, fell dead on Chit-

terne Down. Thomas Saunders, George Waters and Richard Harris were eventually captured, and were convicted at the ensuing Quarter Sessions at Devizes and transported for a term of fifteen years. This monument is erected by public subscription as a warning to those who presumptuously think to escape the punishment God has threatened against Thieves and Robbers.

Mr. Dean, of Imber, was evidently a farmer on his way home from Devizes market, with evidently some harvest money in his pocket. I have heard, from a source which I have long forgotten, a vivid elaboration of this story. On being held up by the four highwaymen Farmer Dean proposed a wager.

"I'll bet," he said "that I'm a better shot than any of you lot."

"Look," he said."We'll throw my hat in the air, and the one who puts most holes in it before it touches the ground takes the money."

They agreed, and the firing began.

"Wait a bit," said one of the highwaymen after a time, as he retrieved the much-battered hat, "The pistols are empty."

"Mine isn't!" said Farmer Dean, "Hands up!"

The story of the subsequent chase reveals one interesting fact. It appears that, contrary to the popular image of highwaymen as cavalier-type gentlemen on horse-back, these robbers were on foot. No doubt Farmer Dean was mounted and doubtless was able to enlist reinforcements during the pursuit. The names and behaviour of the felons would seem to indicate local men, engaged in robbery as a sideline. Probably they had every excuse, living as they did in the aftermath of the Tolpuddle Martyrs.

Building in Mud

20th June 1990

BY May all the farm crops have been sown. Potatoes have been planted. You can almost hear the grass growing in the meadows. Cows eat their fill of it and yield the richest and most abundant harvest of milk in the whole year. Lambs put on weight prodigiously.

Now, in the late twentieth century, silage-making is the main farm activity. Forage-harvesters, more voracious than cows, methodically digest the exuberant surplus of grass and store it for winter fodder. But silage-making is a relatively modern technique. True, it was known more than a hundred years ago, but very few farmers practised it until the 1950s.

So how, in the days beyond the receding horizon, did country folk spend the glorious month of May, before the marathon of hay-making and harvest began in early June? Turnip-hoeing and playing cricket could hardly occupy all their time.

It is, of course, no coincidence that so many traditional holidays belong to May – May Day, Garland Day, Rogationtide, Ascensiontide, Club Festivals, Whitsuntide. But was there anything more? It seemed a fitting question to be put to my long deceased great-grandfather when next I met him under the old apple-tree down the orchard where he used to set up his cider-press.

"Oh yes," he said. "May was the house-building month! When a young working-chap wanted to get married, he had to build his own house, as like as not. May was the best time for that, with its long, light evenings and reasonable weather. So he enlisted a pile of his relations and neighbours – those of them he hadn't fallen out with – and got going...."

Yes, of course. Memory started working for me (for the old technique survived to within my life-time) when a chalk cob garden wall collapsed in one of our winter hurricanes and its owner lamented, "They tell me I'll have to replace it with breeze blocks, because nobody knows how to build with chalk cob nowadays. Do you?"

"Yes, I do." Her face lit up.

"You couldn't make one for me, could you?"

"No, I couldn't, but I can tell you how it's done"

"It's like this. The main ingredient is chalk – rubbly chalk. I emphasise 'rubbly' because if you dig it straight from a chalk-pit it's too rock-like. Ideally you should make a big heap of it in autumn and allow the frost to weather it.

Make the heap as near as possible to where you intend to use it. Mark out the foundations. Depth and preparation are optional. Eighteen inches to two feet are standard, but I have seen much shallower. A professional mud-waller would fill his foundation trench with carefully-placed flints and then take the flint layer a further foot or two above ground. Amateurs in a hurry simply poured in the chalk, especially if they were squatters building where they had no right to be.

The word 'poured' is used deliberately, for the chalk has to be reduced almost to a semi-liquid state – a gooey mess. Old-time practitioners poured buckets of water on it while treading it with their heavy boots. Some of them fastened special iron soles to their boots. As they worked, they also added such ingredients as chaff and horse-hair – something to 'bind' it, as they would say. I suppose any kind of fibrous material would do.

When the rubble had been reduced to the proper constituency, the builders would dig into it and slap it into position on the foundations. I have one of their mud-walling prongs, made for the purpose – a three-tined prong with flattened grains, like a Neptune's trident. Quite heavy.

Each evening they would add a layer of about eighteen inches. Try anything deeper, and the material will collapse under its own weight. Then leave it to set for a day. Examine an old chalk-cob wall and you will be able to trace the eighteen-inch courses – unless, of course, the facing of plaster is still intact.

The obvious way of making the walls smoothly vertical would be to encase them in planking, but old-time builders seem not to have worked that way. I asked great-grandfather William about this, and his explanation was that timber was too expensive. "If they could have afforded timber they would have built their house of it instead of mud!"

So they piled up the chalk rubble, layer upon layer, allowing it to spread as untidily as it chose, until it reached the desired height. Then they sawed it down level with a wooden saw! I don't have one of those saws in my collection of bygones, but I have seen and handled one, years ago.

The one other essential is to give a cob wall a weather-proof hat. If the wall is part of a house, the beams and the thatch provide the cover, but a garden wall must have a roof. Thatch is traditional, but corrugated iron or asbestos or anything waterproof will do. And it must be kept in repair. Once rainwater starts to seep into chalk cob, frost will soon do its disintegrating work, and the wall will collapse.

You then spread the chalk rubble on the nearest ploughed field, as a substitute for lime. Someone finds another use for the flints, and within a few months no-one would suspect that a wall had ever existed there.

Summer Insects

16th June 1989

Bird-watching in July and August tends to be a somewhat futile occupation. All save a few species with gruff voices, such as the wood-pigeon and greenfinch, have ceased their songs, and most of them are moulting and contriving to remain as anonymous as possible. Glimpses of individuals with ragged plumage, retreating into the undergrowth, are all that we are likely to see.

Those of us with catholic interests in natural history, however, can find compensation in the prolific insect life. In my corner of England we are fortunate in having as our neighbours an unsurpassed selection of butterflies, including the magnificent Purple Emperor. In our woods we even have a feature known as Purple Emperor Corner.

When Purple Emperors are on the wing in late July and early August they attract enthusiasts, mostly armed with expensive cameras, from all over England. In the forest one critical weekend I met lepidopterists from Worcestershire, Yorkshire, Norfolk and Shropshire, who considered journeys of two hundred miles or so time well spent, just for a sight of these splendid insects.

The Purple Emperors give the naturalists a run for their money. They are elusive and scarce. At certain times of the day they fly high and powerfully around the tops of tall oaks, but after a period of exercise they will often remain quiescent, on a twig, for hours. The best time to see them is mid-morning, when they are inclined to come down to drink from puddles or explore the delights of fresh horse-manure. Baits of carrion or anything putrid will attract them, and our woodman, who had one alight on his bare arm, says they like him because his is "always sweaty and smelly"!

They also seem to have a predilection for the metalwork of cars parked in warm sunshine. More than once I have taken a half-hour walk in a vain search for Purple Emperors, only to return to the car to find my wife inspecting a specimen on the radiator grill.

These spectacular butterflies (spectacular by British standards though no challenge to the iridescent beauty of many tropical species) are the aristocracy of the summer insect world, but I find the humbler members of that mini-world equally fascinating. This year I have been brushing up my knowledge of bumble-bees and have learned to identify the cuckoo bees, which, as their name implies, lay their eggs in the nests of other bees.

Since we have widened many of the rides in the forest they are margined by a tangle of tall summer flowers, which the uninitiated would call a weed-bed but we value for their attraction for insects. The tall thistles, burdocks, and teazles are humming with life and brilliant with butterfly colour. As a bonus, their seeds are a magnet for goldfinches in winter.

The flowers the insects find most attractive, however, are not necessarily those we most admire. I find one of the most productive flowers to visit in August is the wild parsnip – a rank-scented umbelliferous plant with its tiny yellow flowers arranged in parasol shape. The flower-heads are a miniature world of their own, alive with brightly coloured flies, wasps, and beetles.

They serve, too, to some extent, as a microcosm of the insect population of the entire countryside. This is proving to be an aphid year, perhaps because the winter was too mild to provide a check to these most prolific insects. Greenfly and blackfly have been a menace to gardeners since mid-spring, and farmers have been complaining of aphids attacking their crops.

At the end of June a reader sent me a package of leaves from a garden near Hyde Park (London), with a request to identify a "nasty" sticky substance" on them. "The leaves go patchy white after a few days, as if no photosynthesis is going on and we are very worried about it." I diagnosed honey-dew, which is an exudation of aphids.

In the last weeks of June, when warm sunshine and near-drought prevailed, there were large numbers of aphids in the air. The honey-dew itself is not dangerous to plant life but, being sticky, it attracts all manner of pollution. The leaf pores become clogged and allow fungus diseases to obtain a hold. The break-up of the weather at the end of June (in England we had one of the wettest July's on record) proved a respite, but the aphids now seem to have adapted themselves satisfactorily to rain and wind.

Nowhere are they more abundant than on those wild parsnip plants in the woods. They cover the stems so thickly as to resemble a fuzzy coating. But the hover-flies, with brightly-banded bodies and large glittering eyes, which display themselves on the flowerheads of the wild parsnip, are not there solely for pleasure or even to sip the nectar. They are there to mate and lay eggs, and the aphids are chosen food for their larvae. These grub-like creatures, which resemble pale-coloured slugs, grab the aphids and suck out their soft interior. A single hover-fly larvae needs several hundred aphids to see it through to maturity.

These hover-flies were first in the field, but about a week after I first spotted the aphid infestation the first ladybird arrived. Ladybirds are carnivorous insects which ask for nothing better than a diet of aphids. So the first to arrive lay their eggs in the midst of this almost inexhaustible food supply, and the emerging larvae find their first meal to hand immediately they hatch from the eggs.

The apparently trivial little drama on a flower-stalk in an English wood is not without its significance. It is an example of biological pest control, which, on an international scale, is assuming ever-increasing importance.

Aristocrat of the Downs

22nd July 1990

HANDLING my father's crook and shears the other day reminded me that we are now nearing the end of the sheep shearing season – a calender event which was once of paramount importance on the downland farms of England, though for most of them its significance is now lost. In Wales the shearing was, and probably in some instances still is, a communal effort. Neighbours combined to help each other out. Each farm was dealt with in turn, everyone muscling in, with the womenfolk organising the catering. One of the outstanding social events of the year.

In Wiltshire, though, the tradition was vested in shearing gangs. In recent weeks I have described how the gap between spring sowing and haymaking was filled, in the village calendar, by cottage building and by a series of spring festivals. Sheep shearing also fitted neatly into the gap. The gangs were composed of self-employed labourers who would very shortly be required for haymaking and harvest.

My father, who in due course became a farmer, left school at the age of twelve to become a shepherd boy. In early summer, just about a hundred years ago, he would have been touring a circuit of farms in South Wiltshire with a shearing gang. This week I am going to pass on to you some of his reminiscences as I wrote them down for him in the 1930s.

"There were fourteen of us in our gang," he said; "my

cousin Charlie and myself and the rest all middle-aged men. The area we worked was within fifteen or twenty miles of our village. Most Tuesdays our captain went to Salisbury market and made arrangements with farmers for the week's work. The number of farms we visited each week depended on the size of the flocks, but we usually managed four or five. Ours was one of the stronger companies, and we could make short work of shearing four or five hundred sheep.

"Until Charlie and I joined, the gang walked from farm to farm, but we two had these new-fangled bikes – the first ever seen in our village. The captain was quick to appreciate their advantages. When the gang was making better progress than he had expected, he sent one of us over to warn the next farm, so the sheep could be got into the barn ready for us to begin work as soon as we arrived.

"It was quite a rough hard life. We ate where we worked and slept where we could, usually on a heap of straw in a barn. Our working hours were from four in the morning to eight in the evening. In fact, we woke up at about quarter past three and did four hours' work before breakfast.

Some of the older chaps claimed they would eat a cold breakfast rather than take the trouble to cook, but Charlie and I had a hot one whenever possible. Outside on the downland turf we erected a tripod of sticks to hang our kettle on. By the time we had a fire going and the kettle humming the older men, who had kept out of sight while the work was going on, came sauntering along. We dug rashers out of our rush dinner-baskets, transfixed them with skewers, and gathered in a circle round the fire to toast them.

"Bread and cheese, rashers and onions, were what we mostly lived on. On most farms, though, we could get eggs if we wanted them and then we had to borrow a saucepan from the farmhouse kitchen, for it's difficult to get boiled eggs out of a kettle!"

My father painted a lyrical word-picture of the scene.

"It would be great to be able to turn the clock back just for an hour and have breakfast with the shearers as I did in those carefree days! I can see them now. Bearded, rough-clad men squatting close together on the dewy grass, the dancing flames throwing lights and shadows on their faces. They slowly turn the skewers in their horny, outstretched hands as the fat drops out of the sizzling rashers. The kettle starts to sing and rattle. A lark wakes up and soars, singing, close overhead. In the east the climbing sun is just beginning to shed a little warmth, and all the myriads of dewdrops sparkle in a final blaze of glory before evaporating into nothingness..."

Nostalgia at its best!

My father's apprenticeship as a shepherd coincided with the final phase of the dominance of the sheep in the English farming scene – a dominance which had been unchallenged since the early Middle Ages. On the farms he knew the sheep were the 'golden hoof'. Not only did their wool and meat provide the greater part of a farmer's income, but their droppings, consolidated by their little hooves, supplied the essential fertility for the subsequent wheat crop on the thin chalk soils.

The prosperity of the farm depended on the shepherd, and he knew it. He was the aristocrat of farm workers, and he was certainly an autocrat. Said an apprehensive farmer, steeling himself for an interview with his shepherd, "Ah well, I suppose I must go on up to the sheep and tell old Arthur he's got to cut down on the hay he's givin' 'em. But to tell the truth, I'd just as soon stand up in the field and let en blaze away at I wi' a double-barrelled gun!"

That was my father's ambition as a boy – to be head shepherd of a flock of Hampshire Downs. An Aristocrat of the Downs. But, above all, to live his life with sheep. He never thought he would be a farmer and own a flock.

Poetic Flights

23rd June 1991

A READER exiled in Africa but nostalgic for England in spring, says "Don't you ever feel an impulse to break into verse when you walk in the bluebell woods and listen to the birds' dawn chorus? When last I did so I felt like singing. Can't you treat us to some music in words?"

Who could resist such an invitation! Casting around for inspiration I remind myself of the good old farming maxim: "We can never have too much rain in May," which is as true now as ever it was. Rain is, of course, the prime factor keeping all plant life growing vigorously and so is of special importance at this season. Plants given a good start in life are fortified to cope with prolonged drought later.

By that criterion, May this year was disappointing. Only three days in May brought rain in my part of England, and even that was light stuff rather than a heavy downpour. And for almost the entire month we have shivered under grey, chilly skies and been buffeted by strong northerly winds. No wonder farmers are apprehensive about the months ahead.

However, poets must not permit themselves to be put off by ephemeral adversity.

Here goes:

The beeches creaked: the birches bowed;
The hawthorn clashed their rustling twigs;
The north wind howled a challenge loud,

And all the farmer's little pigs
Cowered in a corner of their sty,
While hens were tossed like flying witches,
And dust-clouds swirled across the sky,
Then dropped into the nearest ditches.
Old Noah leaned against a gate,
His whiskers winnowing passed his ears,
And as he watched the fields vibrate
As though they lived and shook with tears
And saw each single blade of wheat
Drag widely at its anchoring roots,
While wind-waves sped with ripples fleet
Toe upon heel, in wild pursuits,
"The spring be late enough as 'tis,"
Old Noah spat, and shook his head.
"Us don't want much more wind like this;
The wheat be standin' still!" he said.

As a comment on our weather in England this spring that is entirely accurate, and yet I feel that, considered as pure poetry, there is something lacking. I think I know what it is. Re-reading the last two lines I realise that I should have been writing throughout in the vernacular.

That, for me, is of course my native tongue of Wessex, which ought, by rights, to be standard English. It used to be, when Winchester was King Alfred's capital and before its position was usurped by the dialects of Oxford and London. I still dream of the time when I shall switch on the television at breakfast-time and hear the newsreader announce:

"Top of the marnin' to ee! Yer be the tidin's var today..."

It is only a dream, but I do my best to keep our venerable and much-loved tongue alive. With, for example, such topical lines as the following.

The setting is Somerset. A motorist speeding along one of the main roads to the West is held up by a herd of eighty-seven slow-moving Friesians making their way towards the milking shed. He expresses his impatience in the usual manner. Next weekend he gets involved with the same herd in the same place. Here is the soliloquy of the old dairyman driving the herd:

Thee's think thee's seed I once avore, now dussen?
An' thee bist right. An' I've a-heard ee cussen,
A-parmpin' of thee bally ole harn, thee vinger pressed tight on it.
Just 'cos a loose-arsed dummick have wiped her tail athert thee bonnet.
Aye, muck be good var the soil, but it bain't no good for a car,
An' I'll grant ee 'tis waste on a motor-road all mixed up be the tar;
But I wastes me muck, an' thee's waste thee time zo we be even, lack;
An' thee ca'st prectise patience whiles thee's study the small of me back.
Git up there, Daisy! No hookin' there, Dill! or thee milk wun't run down suent,
An' pay no heed to theas gen'leman's words that do vlow zo vast and vluent.
He be driven on, poor zoul, be the urge to git on down to Deb'n,
Not knowin' that tother zide of the haidge be the nearest thing to Heb'n.
There be dillcups, cowslips and granny's bonnets, a-bloomin' in the meddder,
An' there the grazin' cows makes milk var the cheese they zells at Cheddar.
The cuckoo hollers; the vixen youps, an' the zider apples do zet....
Git on where thee's like, but I bides yer – at whoam in Zummeerset!"

Someone to whom I showed these immortal lines commented that she needed a glossary to understand them. Surely not? You don't, do you?

Back to Tea-Kettle Broth

16th October 1988

At the launching party of my book, *The Lost Village*, back in June I indulged in some reminiscences about tea-kettle broth, which was my frequent breakfast in the lean days of the 1920s. It could be described, I suppose, as bread-and-milk without the milk. You crumbled bread into a basin, sprinkled it liberally with pepper and salt, poured hot water on it and ate it with a spoon. Quite tasty, though not perhaps a well-balanced breakfast for a growing boy.

I must add that my mother rang the changes quite efficiently. On most mornings we had bacon, fried in winter and cold in summer, from the cottage pig flitches suspended under the rafters in the kitchen, but tea-kettle broth had to suffice on perhaps two mornings a week. The kitchen fire had to be lit to boil the kettle for the teapot, anyway, so there was economy in it as well. We finished the meal with bread-and-jam – home-made, of course.

The memory was refreshed for me the other week when I learned that the morning cup of tea is definitely bad for us. The warning came from a conference of nutrition experts at Norwich. Specifically, it was given by Dr. Ian Johnson, of the Institute of Food Research, who assured us that the tannin in tea prevents our bodies from absorbing the iron in other foods.

Professor Arnold Bender, Emeritus Professor at London University, backed him up, with the recommendation that, as an early morning drink, orange juice is much better.

"The iron in an egg is virtually not absorbed at all because of interferring substances," he said, "but if you take orange juice with your egg then you will increase the proportion greatly."

Valuable advice, which, incidentally, vindicates me in my liking for boiled nettle-tips as a vegetable in April. Nettle-tips, as I tell my unconvinced wife every spring, are full of iron at a time when our bodies need it most.

But wait! What is this about the breakfast egg? Only a week or so ago we were being warned against eating eggs because of their cholesterol content. Four eggs a week are the maximum compatible with good health, especially for elderly characters, we were advised. Well, when I eat eggs for breakfast I like to have two of them, so that implies eggs on only two mornings a week. What do I have on the other five?

Cereals? But presumably the same objection applies to them as to brown bread. Quite recently scientists have made our blood creep by claims that the insecticides and nitrates applied to farm crops persist longer in the high fibre of brown bread than in white. For years we have been told that brown bread is better for us than white, but apparently it's just as dangerous.

What then? No slice of toast? What! with butter? Not likely. In the matter of cholesterol butter is as lethal as eggs are. Perhaps I should allow myself one slice of white bread, toasted, and plaster it with some of that synthetic vegetable spread which my wife thinks helps her to keep her weight under control. I will eat that with my glass of orange juice. But perhaps it will be as well to check what the vegetable spread consists of: 'Hydrogenated vegetable oil; whey; butter; salt; emulsifiers (monoglycerides, lecithin); whey solids; flavourings; natural colours (annatto, curcumin); vitamins A and D."

I cannot recognise more than half those ingredients, but at the back of my mind are other warnings I have read recently about additives. Are these additives? I don't know. Better, perhaps, to be sure. With my orange juice and white bread I will have just marmalade or jam.

Oh, no I won't. Marmalade and jam are mostly sugar, and I have been warned against sugar if I wish to keep obesity at bay. And honey, of which I am very fond, is, I am assured, just another form of sugar. So, It's back to tea-kettle broth!....

And now, while the water in the saucepan is simmering to the boil, preparatory to receiving two eggs for my breakfast, allow me to initiate you into the mysteries of boiling an egg, the one and only branch of culinary art at which I can claim to be an expert.

Always bring the water to the boil first. Slide the eggs in gently. Allow them four minutes in the boiling water – the three-and-a-half minutes often recommended is not quite enough. When you remove them from the saucepan place them, small and uppermost, in their egg-cups and tap with a spoon to break the shell. This prevents them continuing to cook. Cover with an egg-cosy until the toast is spread, with best butter, and you are ready to eat.

I keep my hand in practice about once a week, when I happen to rise first. On the other days my wife gets the breakfast, and then we have scrambled egg on toast or poached eggs, or fried eggs with rashers and tomatoes, or any other combination of good things which she is adept at devising. And may I offer my felicitations, or commiserations, to those of you who, in the pursuit of longevity, prefer to join the nutrition experts in their breakfast of orange juice and tea-kettle broth.

The Workhouse Bread Van

11th September 1988

A LETTER from my American daughter one morning last week caused me to blink and look again, in disbelief. And that was before I have even opened it. The two orange-coloured 25 cent stamps on the envelope bore the inscription 'Bread Wagon 1880s'. The years fell away like myself gazing at an almost identical bread-wagon (or should I write 'waggon'?) of similar date, not in America but in a clump of bushes on our downland farm in Wiltshire.

It must have been in about 1938. An old-established livery-stable in the town, clearing out its stock of antique horse-drawn vehicles to make urgent room for up-to-date motor cars had approached us in its search for a dumping-site. In due course eight or ten old coaches, landaus, broughams, and other carriages bearing now obsolete and forgotten names were towed to the remote graveyard we provided and there left to disintegrate. They would be worth a mint of money now, but no-one realised that fifty years ago. For a time we used the weatherproof ones for storing tools, binder-twine, and other farm accessories, but during the war residents of a housing estate nearby began helping themselves to bits and pieces for fuel (then scarce), and by around 1945 even the wheels had disappeared.

Like a mongrel at Crufts, there was among the more elegant relics of a vanished era a battered and ramshackle covered van which caused my father to exclaim, when first he saw it, "Surely not? It can't be!"

And he could never make up his mind whether it was indeed the old Workhouse bread-van which featured so prominently in his boyhood memories or one very similar to it.

His father had died, through a tragic mishap, at the age of thirty-three, leaving a widow and three small children, the youngest of whom (my father) was six months old. So my grandmother became a pauper and would have qualified for admission to the district Workhouse if she had not inherited a tiny cottage. The Guardians of the Poor therefore awarded her weekly allowance of five shillings and two loaves of Workhouse bread.

Anyone who has read Ian Anstruther's book *The Scandal of the Andover Workhouse* (published 1973) may be disposed to think that the horrific conditions he exposed ended in 1847. Some of them, such as setting the half-starved inmates to spend thirteen hours a day pounding animal bones into manure, were indeed discontinued, but the system continued to function well into the twentieth century and in the 1880s was as flourishing as ever. The workhouse was a doom-laden spectre in the home where my father was reared. A major disaster, like the breaking of a tea-cup, was sufficient to send his mother into a flood of tears, with the lament, "Now we shall all have to go to the Workhouse."

My father has left some notes of his memories of the Workhouse bread-van, which every Friday used to turn up in our village with the pittances for the paupers.

"Once it had been painted black," he noted, "but many long and dirty years must have elapsed since that event. I knew it as of the same colour as a frock-coat by the time the scarecrow gets it. On the front seat the Relieving Officer and the driver sat bolt upright, a stiff posture which they may have thought added to their dignity but which was, in fact, made essential by reason of a wooden partition rising vertically behind them.

It was the slowest vehicle I have ever seen. I have more than once seen a labourer, dung-spurling in the fields, stop and hold his prong upright at arms length, squinting up and down it in mock gravity to see whether it was moving or not. The horse was a sleep-walker. It was only half-alive, being, like us, dependent for its livelihood on the Guardians of the Poor. With every rib as prominent as a newly-struck furrow it staggered along till it reached the well-known halt at Mrs Cragg's cottage. There, on feeling the reins relax, it stopped dead and immediately fell into a profound sleep.

My father remembered the faded chamois-leather money-bag from with the Relieving Officer distributed the paupers' dole. The Relieving Officer was "not an unkindly old man, though hard work and long acquaintance with the seamier side of life had roughened him. He was paid by the Guardians of the Poor".

"The roll-call ended, the poor-folk flocked out to the bread-van where the driver, a Workhouse inmate, was throwing open the door. Though the driver's hands were noticeably engrimed with dirt, they were at least as well acquainted with soap and water as were those of the other paupers who mixed the dough."

The memory of the Workhouse loaves evidently brought back the smell of them to my father and made him wrinkle his nose. "They were flat and never properly baked," he recalled. "We guessed they were strong on bran and miller's offal, and some swore by sawdust and sour milk. Above all, they stank."

Hungry as they were, the children seldom finished their weekly bread allowance but slipped down from their perches around the table with a blasphemous, "Thank God for a good tea. Amen", rather than touch the disgusting stuff. Fortunately, grandparents and neighbours saved the day on many occasions by sending round to the cottage quartern loaves of home baking.

It seems hardly credible that such conditions prevailed in our English villages at so short a time ago that an American commemorative postage stamp can revive memories of them in a generation still living.

Megaliths at Midsummer

1st July 1990

Once again the police mustered to give Stonehenge, at the summer solstice, the sort of bodyguard normally reserved for royalty. And, once again, in the course of the tourist season more than three-quarters-of-a-million pilgrims will come to gaze at and speculate about the gigantic stones. Their very numbers give cause for anxiety, as their feet wear away the thin turf.

It was very different when first I visited Stonehenge. That must have been in the mid-1920s, soon after Sir Cecil Chubb bought and presented the monument to the nation in 1922. Stonehenge is only about ten miles from my boyhood home, and one summer Saturday my father bundled us all into the old Ford van and took us there for a picnic.

I still have some of the photos we took with our Brownie box camara. My mother and aunt are perched on one of the fallen stones, unwrapping the sandwiches. In the background Salisbury Plain seems completely unpopulated, and there is no barbed wire anywhere.

It must have been much the same fifty years earlier, when old Eliza Harding of Netton – a nearby village which then, incidentally, had a thriving wool store employing thirty or forty people – used on certain days to set up a stall by the lane leading up towards Stonehenge, to serve ale, bread-and-cheese and cakes to drovers and shepherds.

And even earlier, in the eighteenth century, when a

visitor found that 'one, Gaffer Hunt of Amesbury, had built a hut against the upright stone of Mars...and attended there daily with liquors, to entertain the traveller and show him the stones. his cellar was under the great stone next the hut....'

Evidently when Stonehenge began to attract the attention of the intelligentsia visitors were encouraged to chip off bits of stone with great hammers, as souvenirs. Local people had been doing much the same for ages, though in the utilitarian belief that the stone, powdered and tossed down their wells, would discourage toads from taking up residence!

From medieval times onwards writers have speculated about the stones – what was their purpose and, particularly, how did they get there – but there is nowhere any mention of any surviving religious ceremony attached to them. The Order of Druids which holds mid-summer services there nowadays has its origins only in the nineteenth century. And that is curious, for, as a modern writer puts it, 'the Stonehenge circles were orientated by major axes to the midsummer sunrise'.

But the little town of Amesbury and the neighbouring villages have no memories of any rituals or festivities associated with Stonehenge. Only Durrington, three or four miles away, held a festival which featured a dance around a maypole at the Cross Stones in the centre of the village and that was held on May Day, not at midsummer.

Elsewhere in Britain, however, megaliths like those at Stonehenge have significant associations with Midsummer. The Standing Stones of Stanton Drew (near Bath) are said to be dancers turned to stone one Midsummer Eve. The Rollright Stones, in Oxfordshire, were likewise a king and his knights turned to stone by witchcraft on Midsummer Eve. Local people who used to make a Midsummer pilgrimage there, celebrated with dancing and refreshments, used to allocate a man to cut a branch off an elder tree, and they averred that if the trees bled the 'King Stone' moved its head.

Cornish witches used to meet at Midsummer Eve on a rock known as 'The Witches' Rock' near Zennor. Anyone bold enough to venture there at midnight and touch the rock nine times would have good luck for a year. On the South Downs, near Broadwater, a party of skeletons was said to emerge from beneath the roots of an old oak on Midsummer Eve and dance around the tree till dawn, scaring the wits out of anyone who saw them. In the Shetland Isles seals, who were supposed to be bewitched humans, were said to shed their skins on Midsummer Eve and become human again. They spent the short night dancing on lonely sea-rocks until daybreak.

So the links between megaliths and Midsummer and ancient religions can be multiplied...but for Stonehenge, nothing. If the circle was indeed the scene of such bloodthirsty ceremonies as the sacrificial burning of men and animals in wickerwork cages, not the slightest hint can be gleaned from local lore. Stonehenge is austere, aloof, enigmatic, lonely.

As a school exercise I once wrote a sonnet to Stonehenge. Its final lines ran:

Stonehenge sits grey upon the greyish turf,
Grey, grey against the grey November sky,
Grey, on that grey grass ocean, lacking surf,
Far more majestic than in bright July.
For Stonehenge, in its last grey, aged phase,
Needs the environment of fading days.

In short, November is the month into which it fits best.

But now I am not so sure. It occurred to me the other day, as I was watching the crowds of brightly-clad tourists trooping around it and was thinking of the picturesque characters who have to be prevented by force from holding some sort of ceremony there, that that is more like what Stonehenge must have been in its heyday – the centre of crowds of colourful people, not a lonely monument of a grey ocean of grass.

Food off the Wall

7th October 1990

THE large snail, appropriately packaged, that arrived on my desk the other morning, was accompanied by the query, "Is this a Roman snail?"

It was so long ago that I last saw a Roman snail, which is an entirely separate species from our common Garden snail *(Helix aspersa),* that I consulted my reference books, just to make sure. But no, it was just a big specimen of the Garden Snail.

The Roman snail is even larger, with a shell two inches in diameter as compared to one-and-a-half inches for the largest Garden snail, and its shell is cream-coloured, round and noticeably thicker. There is now some controversy as to whether the Roman snails were introduced to Britain by the Romans or whether the Romans found them here when they arrived, all those centuries ago, and being well versed in continental gastronomy quickly added them to their menu.

Whichever is the correct version, they probably improved on nature by establishing snail farms – a procedure more in keeping with Roman character than sending out slaves to collect snails in hedges.

When in the late 1940s and 1950s I was for a time chairman of the Wiltshire County Federation of Young Farmers' Clubs I often found myself conducting inter-club quizzes, quite frequently for radio. Among the questions which cropped up now and again was "What is wall fruit?"

I soon found that knowledge of the correct answer tended to be localised. Clubs from north-west Wiltshire and others ranging as far east as Cirencester and over the Somerset border down the Fosse Way, were quite familiar with "wall fruit". It was their name for snails. Members from clubs in the chalk country farther south had never heard of it.

The logical explanation seemed to be that the snails were found and eaten in districts of late Roman settlement. A British enclave flourished around Cirencester, Bath, and Gloucester for more than a century after the Anglo-Saxons had over-run most of the rest of southern England . For the same period the British endeavoured to keep control of the Fosse Way, that great road which ran diagonally across Britain from Lincoln to near Exeter. And when I began to look into the matter I found that villagers living south from Bath to Ilchester knew about 'wall fruit'. Also on the Mendips, in the vicinity of the Roman mines.

Perhaps an equally important factor is that this is

limestone country – a countryside of stone walls. In the years when I came to know it intimately it was common practice to collect snails for culinary purposes from stone walls, especially around old gardens. I do not know what proportion of the snails were true Roman snails, most of the villagers did not differentiate between them.

With these thoughts fresh in my mind I had a conversation with a colleague who engaged in reminiscences of a remarkable old man who died at the age of ninety-five some ten years ago. He was born at Paulton, in the Somerset coal-fields near Radstock, and, leaving school at the age of eleven, went to work in the pits. Self educated, he later had quite a distinguished career and had a great reputation in his district.

About snails, "he told me that on Sunday mornings miners would search stone walls on the Mendips for snails on their way to the pub. On arrival, they placed the snails on the fire bars and ate them when they were thoroughly roasted. This would have been during the winter, when the snails were hibernating."

Incidentally, snail farming is developing as a new industry in Britain. I know of several in my own district. A friend who has been involved in running one tells me that, here again, Roman snails are not essential; he has worked with English, French and some huge African ones. Far from being kept in darkness, as I would have suspected from my observations of snail habits, they require the equivalent of eighteen hours of daylight per twenty-four. And they have to be kept in a humidity of eighty per cent. I imagined that they probably needed a constant supply of fresh lettuce, but instead they are fed on a proprietary meal mix.

Talking of snails reminds me of Octo, an Aylesbury duck my brother and I had as a sort of pet when we were boys.

He was called Octo because he was the only survivor from a brood of eight. Perhaps because he was lonely, he attached himself to us, and more particularly after first being initiated into the joys of gardening.

One day we were given the task of rebuilding a section of the rockery, and Octo came along to help. Suddenly his sharp eyes alighted on a snail, attached to a rockery stone. He pounced, and from that moment became an addict. It was sufficient for one of us to walk into the garden with a gardening tool; Octo was there, chattering hoarsely and excitedly.

Sometimes we deliberately went snail-hunting for him, turning over stones and logs to see how many snails he could eat, but although on several occasions we totted up twenty or thirty we never reached the limit of his capacity.

Coming to the aid of the injured party

3rd November 1991

A SASKATCHEWAN reader expresses interest in my recent article on birds and animals that tolerate each other's presence but then asks, "Have you ever known one species come to the aid of another?" He then proceeds to give a remarkable instance of this:

> Before coming to Saskatchewan, I lived in Hamilton, Ontario, on the western point of Lake Ontario, in the end suite on the fourth floor of an apartment. Immediately off the balcony stands a tall poplar tree in which nest a pair of Baltimore orioles, a beautiful bird with a lovely song. High above the ground, they were at the height of my balcony. I looked for their return every year and watched them nesting only a few yards away.
>
> One afternoon I heard them making a terrific din, far removed from their usual warble. I went out on the balcony and saw the pair frantically dive-bombing a large black squirrel which was making its way up the tree towards their nest. It ignored their harsh cries and their wings as they swooped and struck at its head. Their cries grew more strident as the squirrels got to within a couple of feet of their nest.
>
> I had reached for an empty flower-pot to throw at the squirrel when I was astonished at what hap-

pened next. Down at ground level, extending out from the back of the building, is a roof which covers the parking area. It is not a closed area, for the sides are open, and it shelters several dozen common English sparrows, which nest in the rafters, feed on the ground, and very rarely ever fly higher than the roof. To my amazement, a squadron of seventeen sparrows suddenly flew out from under the roof – I counted them – and rose straight in a body to my end of the roof, now circling. They flew in formation directly to the poplar tree, where they immediately began to dive-bomb the squirrel, in groups of two or three, one after the other.

The squirrel kept going but could not resist so sustained an attack and, after a couple of minutes, turned tail and beat it down the tree. Once he began to flee the sparrows regrouped in the air. They did not light in the tree but flew straight back down to the parking area and disappeared under it. The exhausted orioles then disappeared into their nest and did not emerge for an hour or so.

Their distress call is certainly far removed from their song. I heard it while inside the apartment, recognised it as something wrong, and went out to investigate. But have you ever heard of one species of bird responding to the distress cry of another?

No, I don't think I ever have, though I think that it happens with certain communal-nesting sea-birds. For instance, let a predatory skua gull appear in the middle of a nesting colony of terns and I imagine the entire colony would take alarm, regardless of which species of tern was immediately threatened. However, the nearest parallel that I have come across concerns a dog and a cat of my

acquaintance. I believe I may have related it before, but it will bear repetition.

Some years ago I sold a house in which I had been living, and , as the new resident was a relation of ours, we decided to leave our cat behind. They had a dog, but the dog had been used to living with a cat and the cat had been living with our dog, so each was used to sharing quarters. As a matter of fact, they settled down quite amicably and took very little notice of each other.

About a week after the move a big dog came into the garden from next door and, finding a strange dog in residence, pitched into it. An almighty rumpus ensued and people came running. So did the cat. Spitting and with talons extended, she made straight for the intruder and, before anyone else could act, landed on his back. The boxer, disconcerted, left attacking the dog and fled back to his own territory, the cat in hot pursuit. It never ventured into the garden again. The newly resident dog retired to the kitchen and remained there, cowering, for an hour or two; the cat proceeded to wash herself.

Now the more you think about this the odder it seems. Here was a cat answering a cry for help not only from an animal of another species but for help against an animal of the same species as was being attacked. If it had been two cats ganging up against a dog it would at least have been logical. And the fact that the dog and cat concerned had been living together for only just over a week makes the incident all the more remarkable. Clearly the bond between the cat and the dog was their home; each had accepted that the other had come to share it and resented the intruder.

Come to think of it, the most fertile source of examples of animals reacting in defiance of the species instinct is when one of the species is human. From the days of Romulus and Remus, fostered by a she-wolf, to dolphins that deliberately play with humans and rescue them if they get into difficulties, instances abound. Pumas are credited with saving the lives of lost children: films of sea-lions in the Galapagos Islands show the animals enjoying a frolic with humans; examples are known of deer soliciting the aid of humans in freeing their young from a snare.

In a perfect world in which mutual trust prevailed there would be many similar instances of humans using their superior technical abilities to rescue our fellow creatures from scrapes into which they had been tempted.

The Parish Lantern

4th November 1990

A READER who moved from England to Newfoundland some six years ago is intrigued by the traditional ideas around which many of his rural neighbours plan their lives. He is particularly impressed by the importance attached to phases of the moon and wonders whether I still pay any attention to them – or, if not I myself, whether my great-grandfather did.

When next I had an opportunity, I discussed the matter with Great-grandfather William, who naturally knew far more about it than I did. The conversation ended with Great-grandfather noticing my yawning and commenting, with a deliberate airing of some of the dialect words we had mentioned: "Ah, well, 'tis up the wooden hill and into blanket-land for you, my lad. So now you'd best be getting along and straming on avore, for 'tis a bit of a jant back home. 'Tis getting dimpsey already, and it'll soon be drapping dark; and then you'll find yourself traipsing home along by the light of the Parish Lantern...."

Some of the words were new to me – I believe they were Devonshire rather than Wiltshire – but I was familiar with the Parish Lantern, the moon. That was a common enough expression in our village before the war. Come to think of it, it was an accurate description of the moon, for artificial lighting for us was confined to indoor oil-lamps, candles, lanterns and latterly, primitive electric torches – nothing anywhere near illuminating the entire parish.

My Newfoundland informant notes that his neighbours refer to 'the light of the moon' when the moon is waxing or full, and to 'the dark of the moon' when it is waning. Great-grandfather knew those expressions. He knew too that you cut fence-posts in 'the light of the moon' if you wanted them to last long, but firewood in 'the dark of the moon'. My correspondent surmises that it could be logical to argue that trees contain the maximum amount of sap when the moon is full – hence the fence posts lasting longer, and the firewood drying out quicker when the moon was waning – that is, assuming that the moon has any effect on the flow of sap in trees.

Another Newfoundland belief is that farm animals should never be castrated in "the dark of the moon": nor should pigs be slaughtered when the moon is waning. My father, who was the village pig-killer among his many other activities when I was a boy, was always busiest in the first fortnight of the moon. Few cottagers would have their pigs slaughtered when the moon was waning, for fear that the meat would go bad. Similarly, most garden seeds had to be sown just before the new moon or in the few days immediately after it.

To that rule, however, there were three exceptions. Beans, peas, and onions had to be sown when the moon was waning. Inexplicable, but there are still plenty of gardeners who observe the rule. Sometimes I find myself following it, arguing with myself that, as I have a whole month to choose from, I may just as well 'sow by the moon', in case there is anything in the old 'superstitions'.

Great-grandfather testified that hedges were normally laid when the moon was waxing, but I have my reservations on that score, because I doubt whether hedgers knocked off work for a fortnight when the moon was waning.

It is still widely believed that the wind, floods, and water levels in wells are controlled by the moon. That seems reasonable enough, for the lunar force which causes the ocean tides is felt by every drop of fluid on earth. The connection of the moon with the wind is rather more abstruse, but countrymen and seafarers must long ago have noticed that the south-west wind brought lashings of rain, with accompanying floods, when the autumnal winds held sway.

Seeing that our bodies are composed largely of water it is not unreasonable to argue that we too may be affected by phases of the moon. There is, in fact, ample evidence to link certain types of lunacy with the lunar rhythm. And some authorities link the female menstrual cycle with the moon.

Great-grandfather's memory, however, took him back to something more primitive and elemental. For instance, he remembers Great-grandmother Elizabeth carrying a parasol when walking in the woods in the moonlight (a detail which I used in my recent novel, *The Secret Lane*). Great-grandfather thought it was just to ward off ill-luck.

Which brings us to the concept of the moon as a powerful supernatural entity. Undoubtedly in ancient times, perhaps even before the building of Stonehenge, the moon was worshipped as a goddess (always, incidentally, as a goddess, never a god). So you should never neglect to bow or curtsey three times to the new moon, gyrating between each bow. After this tribute you may ask favours, especially if you are female, such as advice about love and marriage and also business deals.

Or you can cure warts, by addressing the moon reverently and reciting, "Moonie, Moonie, take my warts away." Silver money (if there is such a thing now) should always be turned at the first sight of a new moon. You should never point at the moon.

And, of course, everyone knows you should never see a new moon through glass. A lovely old neighbour of mine always observed this rule strictly, instructing us to call her if she was indoors, so that she wouldn't be looking though window glass. But she always kept her glasses on when she went outside!

Alternative way of life

13th October 1991

THE plague of voles which I referred to earlier in the summer proved to be patchy, though where they did occur they were present in strength. A neighbour caught (and released a mile or two from home!) well over a hundred in his small garden. And in the same area a few weeks ago I came across a party of stoats who were doubtless attracted by the presence of such bountiful prey.

There were a female and four young ones, almost as big as their mother, leaping and bounding along, a pack of pirates to strike terror in the heart of any vole. The vole population of that district will soon be back to normal. For in addition to being naturally blood-thirsty these stoats, to maintain their high level of activity, need to kill and eat every day; they die of starvation if they have to go more than two days without food. As a matter of fact, starvation is the main cause of death in stoats.

Spare a thought for the mother stoat who reared this brood. She did it entirely unaided by the male, whose sole interest in life is fathering more offspring. After nursing them for five weeks in an abandoned rabbit's burrow she introduced them to the outside world and then, for the rest of the summer, acted as leader of the lively pack. Those which I saw had evidently suffered casualties in their wanderings, for the normal quota of young is six or more. By the end of the season she has exhausted herself in

hunting and catching prey for the youngsters and protecting them from the perils of the way. Small wonder that she has burnt herself out; the chances of her surviving into another year are no more than fifty-fifty.

The stoat (the long-tailed weasel, as it is known in

America) is one of those animals which has developed the technique of delayed implantation. They mate in spring but the newly fertilized eggs soon stop developing and are retained in the womb in a state of suspended animation for the next ten months, until conditions are exactly right for the pregnancy to be resumed. The males live solitary lives, roaming the countryside and seeking for females with which to mate.

The mother stoats are fertile during the spring nursing period, but so are their baby daughters. So prowling males, after mating with the mothers, drag the still blind female babies out of the nest and mate with them as well! If those babies are to produce young when they are one-year-old then that is their only chance of being impregnated. The babies survive and in due course produce the next generation in the following spring.

A simple calculation will show that the odds are in favour of the female stoat which goes in for maximum production rather than one which takes things easy. The latter produces just two young per year and in consequence manages to live for two years, producing another two young in the second year. The second mother has eight young and wears herself out providing for them, dying in her first winter. But in her life she will have produced twice as many offspring as her sister. And if this tendency to live a shorter life and produce more offspring is inherited, then within twenty years there will be more than a thousand times as many of her descendants as of her sister's.

We humans have based our lives on the principle that it is better to reproduce slowly and live longer so as to leave more offspring in the long run. The stoat, confronted with a short and hazardous future, has chosen to throw everything into the current year's reproduction, regardless of the strain it imposes on the mothers. Each species adopts the strategy which nature dictates.

On September 10th I first noticed Silver Y moths feeding on valerian in my garden. Within the next few days, however, there were literally hundreds about . And later that week I found a clover field in which they must have numbered thousands, flitting from flower to flower.

These were migrants, which must have crossed the English Channel in their myriads, for my corner of the countryside lies a good thirty miles inland and there is no reason to suppose that they were concentrated here. In the same week there occurred a minor influx of Red Admiral and Comma butterflies, and in my clover field there were so many Small Tortoiseshells that I cannot imagine they were all hatched locally. This is one of the biggest migrations of butterflies and moths that I have ever witnessed, and fortunately the weather has been so kind to them that they are still here, a fortnight after the invasion. Presumably most of them will perish without leaving progeny, but it is good that they have been able to enjoy weeks of sunshine after their tremendous journey.

Meantime one would never have suspected that we were eight million birds short, including one million migrants, as a result of bad weather in spring. Certainly there was some interference with nesting, especially locally, but that seems to have been compensated for by better conditions in the North, to judge by the numbers of swallows and martins passing through on southward migration. The weather has been such that the birds have tended to dawdle, remaining in chosen localities for days on end, but the fact is that over the past few weeks I have seen more of them than for several years and still they keep coming, scores upon scores of them.

Scared of thunder

8th September 1991

"OUR young, Golden Labrador, recently acquired, goes frantic in a thunderstorm," writes a Worcester correspondent. "We just don't know what to do with him. Can you suggest anything? We understand that this is quite a common reaction."

Yes, it is. Sam, our Pekinese, surrenders to panic when the thunder starts. We admit him to our bedroom, with the light switched on and us trying to comfort him, and he is still scared out of his wits. He howls and whimpers, he paws frantically to get out, or to get in, and when the storm begins to recede he creeps under the bed and stays there for the rest of the night.

Most of the other dog-owners tell much the same story. They would have been able to sleep through the storm themselves, they say, if it hadn't been for the wretched dog! "In the end he got us so thoroughly awake that we got up and made a cup of tea!" is a lament I hear quite frequently. It is true that not all dogs exhibit the same extreme reaction. One correspondent says of her late fox terrier that, "she didn't kick up a row but used to tremble violently and salivate copiously," and that, I think, is typical of the reaction of a dog used to being left to fend for itself. Hardly any report their dogs as being completely unmoved.

It is not just the noise and the bright flashes. Now that Sam has become familiar with thunderstorms he can detect the approach of one before we can. When on a hot, humid day he follows us around, panting and looking beseechingly to be picked up, we suspect a coming thunderstorm, and sooner or later it arrives. And this is understandable, for a meteorologist has explained to me that even on a fine, clear day the atmosphere is charged with electricity. At ground level the charge is negative, but in the air it is positive, and it increases by 120 to 150 volts for each metre (or yard) of height. When a violent storm develops, this electric charge increases at a prodigious rate.

When it reaches 500,000 volts a flash of lighting occurs. With all that electricity in the air it is no wonder that animals react to it.

So, of course, do we, though not so intensely. Instances have been known of men finding their hair standing on end just before seeing a lightning flash. And no wonder! Lightning appears to flicker because the electrical discharge follows the same path twice! The charge strikes the earth at a speed of about sixty miles per second but then surges back up the same path. The path it follows is only a few millimetres in diameter but within that narrow space the temperature reaches up to 30,000 degrees Centigrade. As this immensely powerful charge disperses in the clouds we hear its effects in the form of thunder.

Until about one hundred and fifty years ago lightning was the only form of electricity known to most people. There are a lot of things we still don't know about lightning, but our ancestors knew less, and they had every reason for alarm at such a powerful and unpredictable force. Old customs linger.

Some country folk, for instance, always get up and get dressed during a thunderstorm at night. This behaviour may have a logical origin, for in the days when most cottages were thatched there would be little time to dress if the place were struck by lightning. Others, though perhaps not many nowadays, open at least one door to the outside, and this too may have a sensible explanation. It is a precaution against ball lighting or 'fire-balls', which enter a room and float about in an erratic manner. Normally they do no damage, even if they touch a person, but occasionally they burst with a loud explosion. It would be quite reasonable to open a door to allow one to stray outside, especially by someone who had seen one.

It used to be common practice for a housewife to cover with cloths all mirrors and other furniture with shining surfaces when a thunderstorm was imminent and hurriedly to hide away cutlery in drawers. The belief was that bright surfaces attracted lightning. When umbrellas first became fashionable a type was marketed with a metal lead dangling from the rear and trailing along the ground. A personal lightning conductor! As for mirrors, it was said that they were covered during a thunderstorm because if you looked into a mirror while a storm was raging you would see the Devil looking over your shoulder!

A reader asks whether it is true that a thunderstorm will never cross a river. Not entirely, but there is an element of truth in it. A thunderstorm will follow a course dictated largely by the ground temperature, and the ground temperature is highest over ploughed ground and built-up areas, not so high over woodlands, and lowest over water. Therefore a storm will tend to avoid crossing a river and will follow the enclosing hills, though that is not an invariable rule.

I haven't had many reports about cats but gather that they are similarly affected, or at least some of them, as are horses. In a recent thunderstorm a valuable horse of my acquaintance was so frightened that it dashed against a barbed-wire fence and did itself damage requiring the attentions of a vet. I wonder whether wild animals react in the same way? I doubt it, because birds seem not a bit worried by all the noise and flashes. But has anyone observed in a thunderstorm the reaction of wild animals? Say deer?

I asked a neighbour how his two-year-old reacted and was told that he crowed with delight and said, Bang! Bang! So evidently small children are not naturally terrified by all the rumpus. When they show fear they have caught the reaction from grown-ups!

Old time Courtship and Marriage

22nd September 1991

THE delightful 'shower' which formed part of the celebrations at my son's wedding in rural Manitoba some twenty years ago has regrettably declined, a Winnipeg correspondent informs me. It has, in fact, deteriorated into a women-only party. "We all sit around someone's living room and play ridiculous games, watch the bride-to-be open her presents and then have tea."

"One game" is to have each guest attempt to trace her hand on a piece of paper lying on the floor. No knee bending. While this is going on a snitch in a corner is writing down every word each contestant says. This catalogue is then read out, to great hilarity, as these are the words the bride is supposed to utter on her bridal night. Such as "Oof, I can't reach!" or "Oh, my God! My back!"

Manitoba is also the proud initiator, or practitioner, of a custom called a 'social'. This is a co-ed affair (thank goodness!), a dance to which tickets are sold. The parents of the bride and groom, and some long-suffering aunts and uncles, are present, but mostly it's the young crowd, and the music is loud and rocky. This is a great money raiser, mostly from the sale of liquor, and no young Manitoban would feel properly married without a social."

Well, I suppose that the age-old custom of 'bundling' is now obsolete, though it survived in some out-of-the-way places when I was young. Imagine life in an isolated and somewhat primitive agricultural community. In summer work occupied every daylight hour and left little time for courting, but how to spend the long, dark winter evenings, when a gale raged outside? A young man might be invited into his girl-friend's, there to spend the evening engaging in polite social conversation with a swarm of younger brothers or sisters, but if he jibbed at this how else could he conduct a courtship?

The obvious solution was to go to bed and that was what happened. The elememtary precaution of requiring the couple to remain fully clothed was taken, or, alternatively, to be 'bundled' in a sack, but if they managed to wriggle out as soon as left alone that was a risk that had to be taken.

Even more open was the custom of agreeing to be 'Lammas brother and sister'. This became localised in association with Kirkwall, in Orkney, which traditionally held an eleven-day fair at Lammas-tide. A row of sheaves was laid out on a barn floor for lodging for young people of both sexes who had nowhere else to go. For this reason a couple who had agreed to be a 'Lammas brother and sister' were allowed full marital rights for a year, without restriction, but on the understanding that at the end of that period the transaction had to be confirmed.

In a recent article I introduced the character of a 'bidder' who, in the days before the introduction of the penny post, used to be in demand for announcing forthcoming weddings. A correspondent tells me that after the ceremony guests so invited used to race on foot or horseback to the reception for prizes. She quotes an advertisement for a Public Bridal, "when the couple will be glad to see their friends and all who may please to favour them with their company: for whose amusement there will be various races for Prizes of different kinds; amongst others, a saddle and bridle; a silvertipped hunting horn for hounds to run for."

As to expenses towards the end of the 'bridewain' the bride sat enthroned with 'a pewter dribbler in her lap', collecting contributions, which came pouring in, 'as thick as hail'. For a poorer couple the request might be for a supply of seed corn or potatoes, which was seldom refused.

In her book, *The Folklore of the Isle of Man*, Margaret Killip, writing in 1975 says,

> Life is not now always recognisably Manx, far from it, but from time to time there is an upsurge of insular sentiment and it is decided to hold some 'Manx' event. A Manx wedding is the most popular of all because it is the most spectacular. People will flock there in hundreds.

Its chief attraction is the wedding procession, in which almost everyone can take part; headed by the bride riding on horseback with her father to the church, then the bridesmaids and groomsmen following two by two, and those not occupying the chief roles joining in as wedding guests....The scene is much as at an early nineteenth century wedding, a walking wedding perhaps, when anyone who was met by the wedding party on the way to church had to join in the procession and go along with it until the bridegroom gave them leave to go on their way.

The Autumn Cornucopia

11th November 1990

I HAVE been chestnutting. Readers in France, Italy and other well-favoured lands where chestnut trees grow as freely as weeds would regard mine as a rather poor little nutting expedition, for England is not really a chestnut country. Sweet chestnut trees grow well and produce useful timber but the nuts tend to be small and stunted. In a spiny-cased cluster of four, which is how they are often arranged, only one of the four will contain a fully-developed nut, and that not a very big one. The rest will be flat travesties of nuts – nuts that started with the right pattern but which never properly filled out. I enjoyed my chestnutting, though , I went home with a plastic shopping bag more than half full and so now have an adequate store of nuts for roasting on the fire-bars on winter evenings. My wife has cook-books containing recipes for using chestnuts, but I dare say it is nostalgia that makes me prefer roasting them in the old-fashioned way, as we used to when we had an open hearth.

Apart from extensive plantations in Kent and Sussex, where they were traditionally grown for providing hop poles, sweet chestnut trees are not very plentiful in England. In the forest reserve of 1,750 acres in which I have a special interest, however, we have several acres of them, mostly between fifty and a hundred years old and in a year like this, when the trees are loaded with nuts, there are far more than enough for my requirements.

That is just as well for I have plenty of competition. Squirrels, mice, and every woodland rodent assemble for the feast, but the most assiduous of all are the deer, of which we have both fallow and roe. As they are primarily nocturnal I have seldom seen them at their meal, but almost every day I see evidence of their activities. They open the prickly husks with their sharp hooves, creating small quagmires under the chestnut trees.

This autumn they have plenty of choice, for the woods and hedges have produced a cornucopia of good things. Earlier I commented on the huge crops of hawthorn berries, beech-mast, crab apples, and maple seeds which seemed to be developing. More recently supplies have been augmented by acorns, hips, hazel-nuts, blackberries, spruce cones, honeysuckle berries, sloes, and, of course, sweet chestnuts, as well as scores of species of herb and grass seeds.

Never have I seen beech trees more heavily laden with nuts. In our wood of several millions of beeches there should be ample provision for the bird population of the entire district for the winter. While the nuts were on the trees they were enjoyed chiefly by tits and chaffinches, but now they are falling fast, splitting their husks and revealing their kernels in the process, they are available to a much wider range of creatures. Deer, squirrels, rabbits and mice all love them. Pheasants gobble them greedily, as do pigeons, collared doves and greenfinches.

So would any pigs which had access to them. Under the old open-field system of agriculture which prevailed for a thousand years, perhaps more, the beech-nut harvest was of prime importance to the village swineherd. He would have rejoiced to see such a harvest as we have this year. So would his superiors, for as far back as the reign of King Alfred (in the ninth century) the lord of the manor, who in many instances was the king, would claim a levy on the additional weight put on by pigs turned loose to forage on the woodland crops in autumn.

And how was that measured? By the thickness of the back fat, as against a standard measurement assumed for the period before the autumn harvest. And still, in 1990, back fat measurement is calculated, though nowadays the back fat can be measured electronically in live pigs instead of having to wait until the pigs are killed.

Incidentally, I reckon the frugally-minded could save quite a bit of garden peanut expenditure by collecting beech-nuts under the great trees. Beech-nuts are highly nutritious, being so oily, that in the Mediterranean they were not so long ago used extensively for extracting oil, to be used both in cookery and as a fuel. At present they can be gathered by the bucketful and might well be more wholesome for garden birds than peanuts, some of which were suspect in quality last year.

*   *   *

From a reader in central France a letter introduces two of the less common contributors to the autumn cornucopia:

> A lady across the way from us has a fine hornbeam tree, perhaps sixty feet high. She said to us the other morning, 'Have you seen my Golden Delicious?' Pointing to the top of the tree she showed us the fruit in question – two very large ripe pumpkins! She is now faced with two problems – whether to call the fire brigade or leave them and risk being crowned by a fruit of several kilos weight. As the plant invaded her garden from next door, the problem of who owned the pumpkins also arises. And what is the altitude record for pumpkins!?

My correspondent also reported that sunflowers are taking over as a new crop in this part of France, "It's fascinating to watch them follow the sun across the sky during the day, but what puzzles me is why they should always be facing east when they die! I would have thought westward would be more logical. Why east?

This is a new phenomenon to me. Readers may like to have a go at an explanation.

The Moon and the Sun

23rd December 1990

PAYING a periodic visit to a badger sett in mid-November I noted the heaps of dry grass, dying bracken, and fallen leaves around the main entrances. Three days later all had vanished. They were the badgers' harvest, collected for winter bedding.

Badgers do not hibernate, in the strictest sense of the word. Unlike dormice, they do not experience a period of complete torpidity, when the body temperature falls so low that the animal appears to be dead, its muscles rigid and its heartbeat almost indistinguishable. But bad weather will keep a badger underground for weeks. In autumn it fattens up to the extent that its weight increases by more than fifty per cent, and in the dark days it lives off its accumulation of fat.

These musings were prompted by the numerous letters that landed on my desk in response to my recent article on moon lore. Several of them were concerned with the names and characteristics of the autumn moons. The first of the three is the Harvest Moon, which this year was full on October 4th. It derives its name from the fact that, due to certain complex astronomical reasons, it rises at approximately the same time every evening when it is near full. In times past it gave sufficient light for gathering the last sheaves from the harvest field. Barley sheaves mostly.

The next autumn moon is the Hunter's Moon, which this year was at its full on November 2nd. This moon too offers the advantage of being at its zenith for a longer time than usual when it is full. In the middle of its month, in fact, it rises less than twenty minutes per night later for a fortnight. Harvest is now safely over, however, or should be, so the country folk whom it benefits are hunters.

But also badgers. I have heard it called the Badgers' Moon, by which name I believe it is commonly known in the Highlands of Scotland. The reason, of course, is that badgers take full advantage of it in gorging themselves and in collecting their winter bedding.

I have never heard any specific name for the December moon, doubtless because it has no claim to supplying extra hours of evening light, though throughout the nights it does service as the Parish Lantern. But perhaps readers under other skies do have a name for it?

A reader in the world of the theatre tells me he had recently been directing at the International Theatre in Vienna the musical *Quilters,* which is an epic panorama about the lives of women in the pioneer days of the American West. "One scene", he says, "deals solely with the assertion that in building a log cabin one should lay floorboards only in the dark of the moon. If you do so under a waxing moon they will immediately curl up and warp, and the prairie dandelions will grow up between the cracks."

Incidentally, he takes issue with me that there was a natural tendency to regard the moon as female. In England, he says, that is true, but in many other languages (and he gives an impressive list of them) the moon is masculine.

From the moon we turn to the sun. Recently I quoted a query from a French reader who asked why the sunflower turns its face towards the east when it dies.

From France another reader points out that there are two distinct species of sunflower. One, *Helianthus,* derives its name from the similarity of the flower to the sun and does not necessarily turn towards it. It faces the sun in the mornings but does not follow it during the heat of the day. The other, the *Heliotropium,* does apparently turn towards the sun.

A Canadian reader, however, supplies me with a convincing scientific explanation which I quote in full:

> Anyone who has kept house plants is familiar with the phenomenon of plants growing towards the light. The sun's rays inactivate a plant growth hormone so that the side exposed to the sun does not elongate, whereas the shaded side continues to do so. Sunflower flower buds 'follow the sun' from east to west

during the day for the same reason. During the night, however, when the inhibition of this plant growth hormone production ceases, they slowly twist back to face east again by morning. By the time that flowering starts and the yellow ray flowers on the outside of the head are exposed, the heads are usually too heavy to move, and so from then on they face east all day.

That is why a field of sunflowers that has been sown east to west makes such a dramatic picture when seen from the east in the morning. Anyone looking at a field of sunflowers in bloom from the west will see only the backs of the heads, with only an occasional individual looking the wrong way.

My informant in this instance is a world-famous expert on sunflowers, though I am not at liberty to mention his name. And, incidentally, farmers in southern England are taking a renewed interest in sunflowers as an alternative crop to cereals on arable farms. I saw several fields in full bloom last summer. They cater for the edible oils market, the seeds containing between thirty and forty per cent of oil, while the seed residues, after the oil extraction, are moulded into a useful cake for livestock. There is also quite a demand for sunflower seed for feeding garden birds.

Under the Fish and Over the Water

24th February 1991

OVER the past ten or twelve years community plays have become quite popular in the West Country. The idea behind the movement, which was started by Ann Jellicoe at Lyme Regis in 1978, is to involve as large a slice as possible of the populace in producing a play of local interest under the management of a core of professionals.

One such play was performed two years ago in a village near my home (Farley) on the occasion of the tercentenary of the church. The action naturally took place in the church itself, with the leading actors moving about among the audience and involving them as much as possible. This, though was a small event compared to some that have been staged in towns big enough to rope in two thousand participants.

Last autumn it was the turn of the Wiltshire town, Bradford on Avon, which put on a community play with the evocative title,*Under the Fish and Over the Water*. That is a conundrum I remember well from the days when, as quizmaster, I conducted contests between teams of Young Farmers' Clubs. If you were 'under the fish and over the water', where would you be? Answer – at Bradford on Avon. The reference is to a bridge, over the Avon, on which stands a little stone cell surmounted by a weather-vane in the form of a fish.

'The Bradford Gudgeon' is the local name for the fish, though goodness knows why such an undistinguished

species was chosen. The date and original purpose of the building are unknown, though some writers have thought that it was, or was on the site of, a medieval chapel. However, the present building was certainly there in the 1740s when it was in use as a lock-up. One of John Wesley's preachers was incarcerated there for a night in 1757 and so was able to claim, like so many other prisoners, that he had spent a night, 'under the fish and over the water'.

Two hundred years ago most parishes in the kingdom had a lock-up like the one under the Bradford Gudgeon.

They were designed chiefly for local offenders and were much patronised by those arrested for being drunk and disorderly. As this was a kind of occupational hazard for regular customers of ale-houses, characters unlucky enough to be apprehended could rely on their friends outside to make their captivity at least tolerable. Barred windows and keyholes offered opportunities for supplying beer even if escape were impossible, though there were numerous instances of prisoners escaping via rotten floors and windows.

Interested to know what it was like to be locked up in a parish lock-up, I discovered a letter written by William Hitchens to John Wesley about his experience at Bradford on Avon. He wrote:

> Reverend and Dear Sir," he wrote..... "at Bradford in the evening I was pressed for a soldier. I must go to the Round House the little stone room at the side of the bridge; so thither I was conveyed by five soldiers. There I found nothing to sit on but stone, and nothing to lie on but straw; but soon after a friend sent me a chair on which I sat all night. I had a double guard, twelve soldiers in all, two without, one in the door and the rest within. My body was in prison but even there I found some work to do for God; I had a fair opportunity of speaking to them that durst not leave me, and I hope it was not in vain.

The cell, it will be noticed, was referred to as the Round House, a name commonly applied to lock-ups, whether they were round or not. Other names for them were Blindhouse, Guardhouse, Cooler, Clink, Little Ease and Cowhouse. As a matter of fact, very few were round, though a fine example of a round one is to be found about ten miles from my home – at Shrewton in the middle of Salisbury Plain. It stands by the roadside in the centre of the village and until quite recently was a traffic hazard, though after being partially demolished several times it was moved back several yards into a safer position.

The Shrewton Roundhouse served the useful function of a halfway house between Devizes and Salisbury. After trudging twelve miles or so across the exposed downs the prisoner(s) would be locked in the Round House, which was, unlike some lock-ups, equipped with a wooden bench, while the escorts put up at The George.

Round houses were, or course, not regarded as places of punishment but simply of convenience. People who made nuisances of themselves were locked up there until they could be tried. At one time there were over two hundred capital offences on the statute book. For those who escaped being hanged there were the stocks, the pillory, and the whipping-post, and lock-ups in towns were generally situated near these amenities. In villages they were usually sited centrally, chiefly for the convenience of the constable or watch-man who liked to be near the local tavern on cold nights.

Lock-ups on frequently used routes were emptied as quickly as possible in the mornings, for the parish was responsible for the upkeep of any prisoners. Instances occurred, however, of inmates being frozen to death, and Castle Cary, in Somerset, has the story of a man who was locked up over Christmas, forgotten about, and found dead later.

What happened to William Hitchens after his night "under the fish and over the water"? He was set free when it was discovered that he owned some property. The law said that a property-owner could not be press-ganged for service in His Majesty's Forces!

Getting about in the old days

25th November 1990

MY recent definition, for the benefit of a New Zealand family researcher, of a 'hay-binder' has prompted an Australian correspondent to fire a somewhat similar query at me. "Do you, or does your Great-grandfather, know what a *cab-runner* was?" Both of us can answer Yes: myself from hearsay and he from observation.

Great-grandfather William recalls that coaching inns, and later railway stations, (he lived in the transition period between the two) were frequented by a man of somewhat rascally appearance who offered, for a tip, to take charge of the luggage of a disembarking passenger and stow it in a cab. He then hung around to hear the passenger's instructions to the cabby. Sure enough, when the cab arrived at its destination, there would be the same character, waiting to unload the luggage and so earn another tip.

One supposes that if necessary the man was prepared to run by the side of the cab, a feasible operation on a short journey through town streets, but he much preferred to cadge a ride on the back axle of the cab. A standard design was for cabs and carriages in general to have an exposed back axle. As a boy, in the last days of the supremacy of horse-drawn vehicles I remember often hearing the cry "Whip behind!" shouted by nosy-parkers to inform the driver the boys were cadging a ride at the vehicle's tail. We exploited any kind of vehicle, but it must have been much easier, not to say irresistible, when a convenient back axle was on offer.

We did it, of course, for fun, but for the luggage-handler it was part of his workaday routine. Fortunately for him, most cabs were so constructed that the driver could not see the rear of the vehicle, so for him too the only peril was a cry of "Whip behind!" He hardly deserved the name, *cab runner,* but that is what he was called.

He was, of course, unpopular with cab-drivers, who had no hesitation about plying that whip. Some of them employed that more reliable deterrent of keeping a Dalmatian dog to run between the wheels of the cab.

A few years ago I remember writing of the arrival of a new village neighbour whose family included a Dalmatian dog. It wasn't long before the dog discovered that our village had a flourishing horse population. In particular, it attached itself to a stable of three ponies, whose owners were rather amused at their new acquisition and were happy to encourage it . In due course they also acquired a nice little light two-wheeled trap for use on our country lanes, and the Dalmatian naturally accompanied them on their excursions, trotting between the wheels.

Owners of Dalmatians have told me that the dogs can readily trot along with horses for fifteen or twenty miles a day without tiring. There is a record of a Dalmatian in coaching days who ran with a coach for the fifty miles from London to Brighton for eight consecutive days. There is a suspicion, though, that like the cab-runner, it cadged a lift from time to time.

A handsome spotted dog running behind one's carriage must have added distinction to the outfit, but practical considerations also existed. Within living memory the only form of public transport on Guernsey was horse-buses. The roads being so tortuous and narrow, the buses were accompanied by Dalmatians. For most of the journeys the dogs ran some distance in front of the vehicle, to warn other vehicles and pedestrians of its approach, but on the infrequent wider and straighter stretches they would fall back and run behind the bus.

The belief that the Dalmatian has lost its sense of smell is a myth, but the breed takes little interest in the world of scent, even tending to ignore other dogs. It is also a rather timid dog. I was once told of a Hampshire Dalmatian who, following his master's carriage, was habitually set upon by the village dogs. His owner eventually dealt with the problem by painting black spots on his white bull terrier and letting the animal take the Dalmatian's place as carriage escort. In the ensuing rumpus the village dogs learned a lesson they never forgot! From that time the Dalmatian was left in peace.

The origins of the Dalmatian are unrecorded. They seem to have had no connection with Dalmatia. The fact that seventeenth century Puritans were prejudiced against it as a 'papist dog' suggests a possible Italian origin.

In the West Country we used to call them 'plum pudding dogs'. That sounds like a humorous reference to their spots, but West Country folk used to have a deep-rooted objection to using the word 'spotted'.

No Props Needed

25th September 1988

WE were carting wheat-sheaves, harvesting according to the time-honoured practice of centuries before the combine-harvester took over. Our team consisted of four working in the field and four at the rick.

Frank drove the tractor between the field and the rick, but in the field his place was taken by a schoolgirl, releasing Frank for the heavier task of pitching sheaves on to the waggon for loading. The other pitcher was Albert, a pensioner, and two girls were on the trailer, shaping the load.

At the rick seventy-year-old Arthur and myself were the centre of operations. I was the official rick-builder, while Arthur had the skilled job of passing them to me. George, a man of girth and muscle, had the exacting task of unloading the trailer, tossing the heavy sheaves up to Jeremy, who stood in the 'pitch-hole', and passing them to Arthur.

Rick-building needs a good deal of skill and experience, and Arthur and I were the only two men on the farm who possessed it. Earlier in the day I had strode out the rectangular ground-plan, marking the corners with spars and filling it with a generous layer of loose straw. In the middle I made a tent-shaped 'hile' or stook of upright sheaves. After that was in position it was a matter of concentric placing of sheaves, working outward from the central 'hile'. The butt-ends of the sheaves were always placed towards the edge of the rick, and the sheaves were packed as closely as possible.

The outer edge reached, we then worked back towards the centre, fitting a series of binding layers, with the butt-end of each sheaf resting on the bond of the sheaf beneath. So the work proceeded, layer upon layer, hour after hour. As I moved around the rick I stood on each sheaf immediately I had placed it. Tight packing was essential; loosely-knit ricks were apt to develop unsightly bulges and required propping up, inviting general ridicule.

The roof required a somewhat different technique, the complexities of which can only be mastered by practice. Sufficient to say that a properly constructed roof will keep out any normal rainfall for weeks, though a covering of thatch is desirable if the rick is to stand for much of the winter.

I have been indulging in reminiscences. That is not a description of harvesting last week but of what went on on our farm forty-five years ago. It is based on my notes jotted down at the time.

And yet, in a way, it is up-to-date. For a farmer neighbour, realising that his house will need re-thatching this winter, has grown a few acres of a suitable variety of wheat to provide the thatch. And he nobly acceded to my suggestion that I help him build the rick, just to see whether I still retained the old skills.

'Help' is the operative word. I put in an hour or two one evening and had another session the next day, but when the rick rose to eaves-level I retired. I have no head for heights nowadays. Still, I was pleased to find I had not lost my touch. I gave the rick a good foundation, and when it was finished it didn't need to be propped up by baulks of timber. And I think I may have passed on some useful tips to a new generation of country lads.

The combine-harvester has made most of the old harvesting techniques obsolete, but it cannot cope with thatch. Thatching straw still has to be bound into sheaves, allowed a period of maturing in ricks and then threshed by a machine called a 'reed-comber'. In it each sheaf is held in a position where only the ears are battered by the threshing-drum, leaving the precious straw intact.

The farmer has to make a certain sacrifice of yield to obtain thatching straw of good quality. Most of the modern, high-yielding varieties of wheat are of little use. The standard variety of years ago, the once popular, long-strawed Squareheads Master has long since been superseded. Even Maris Widgeon, which replaced it and which is still grown for the purpose, is no longer listed by most seed-merchants, and thatch-producing farmers have come to rely on exchanging seed among themselves. My neighbour is making do with the variety Aquila, which seems to be reasonably satisfactory.

When I learned farming under my father's tuition, all

those years ago, rick-making was one of the skills I automatically acquired. Others I can think of, offhand, were hand-milking, ploughing with a horse-drawn plough, flat-hoeing, singling, hedging, dung-spurling, thatching, curing the home pig, paunching rabbits, assisting with difficult calvings and lambings, sharpening grasscutter knives, even, to a small extent, 'drowning' (the management of water-meadows). And a fat lot of use any of these ancient techniques are to me now – though one day maybe I shall have the chance of recording them for posterity. Still, it is good to know that rick-making is still in modest demand and has a chance of surviving.

Watering with the foot

23rd August 1990

HALF-DREAMING as I sat in church the other Sunday morning, while the parson ploughed through what seemed to me some rather boring irrelevancies from the Book of Deuteronomy, I had my attention suddenly focussed by an apparently nonsensical phrase.

"Egypt, where though sowedst thy good seed, and wateredst it with thy foot, as in a garden of herbs......"

"Wateredst it with *thy foot*," eh? You don't water plants with your foot! Or do you?

Something clicked in my memory. I was a teenager, walking around his farm in the 1930s with Mr. Ernest Kent, of Homington, in the Wiltshire valley of the little River Ebble. It was a clear, crisp March morning, with the frost lingering as it had for the past three weeks and dominating unchallenged the bare upland fields, but the riverside meadows which we were inspecting were already luxuriant with a crop of fresh young grass, four or five inches tall.

For these were water-meadows, and the channels, brimming and spilling over with gently flowing water, were creating a genial micro-climate. Mr. Kent paid careful attention to each carriage and drain. Presently we came to an empty one. Without even stooping, he pushed aside a turfy clod with the side of his boot, and the pent-up water, released, poured into the channel. He had indeed watered the crop with his foot!

For Mr. Kent was a skilful drowner. He was also a farmer, but somewhere in his youth he had mastered the intricate art of managing a water-meadow, and it continued to give him more satisfaction than all the other farm activities. The shepherd could attend to the sheep, the dairyman to the milking, the carter to the plough, but Ernest would delegate the control of his water-meadows to no-one. And because he was one of the last of the professional drowners the ancient art has become obsolete.

It wasn't his fault, of course. Water-meadows were designed for sheep, and from the 1870s onward sheep farming in the traditional style fell into deep financial trouble in the chalk country of southern England. Water-meadows were an integral part of the old high-farming system under which specialist breeds of sheep fed on arable crops grown specifically for them, manuring the soil as they fed. It was too labour intensive to survive the depression which hit agriculture when the American prairies began to pour their wheat into England.

When the system was flourishing, every river and stream in the chalk country was utilised, from source to mouth, to irrigate water-meadows. At the head of each group of meadows a dam controlled the water-level and created a deep pool. From it ran a series of parallel channels in a grid iron pattern, four or five yards apart. They were at two levels. The water was admitted at the higher of the two and flowed through a channel, known as a 'carriage', along the top of a slight bank.

The flow was regulated so that the water spilled over the rims and trickled down a gentle slope into the 'drains', two or three feet lower. From there it was conducted back to the main channel and so to another hatch-controlled dam, ready to irrigate the next meadow. The effect was to cover the entire corrugated surface of the meadows with a gently moving carpet of clear, spring water.

The irrigation season was from December to March and was against frost rather than drought. Hurdle flocks, notably the Hampshire and Dorset Down breeds, which lambed in early February had lambs of a size capable of taking full advantage of a bite of young spring grass by the end of March.

At its height, the system was so popular that the supply of water had to be strictly controlled. Each farm with water-meadows by a chalk stream was entitled to flood them between certain set dates, with penalties enforced against anyone trying to cheat. What we in our conservation-minded age would consider a bonus was the wonderful haven the meadows offered to wildlife in hard winter.

So every day, when his meadows were flooded, Ernest Kent walked through his water-meadows, adjusting the water levels with a spade or with his foot. As in the irrigated herb gardens by the Nile, as the Book of Deuteronomy describes. And from April to June his lambs flourished and fattened on the lush grass, ready for the early market around midsummer.

It was essentially a system based on sheep, for they alone could graze in the meadows without damage to the water channels. The larger, clumsy hooves of cattle could quickly damage them – which is exactly what happened when sheep became unprofitable and chalkland farmers switched to dairy farming.

Apart from requiring the services of an expert drowner, the meadows were labour-intensive in that, if they were mown for hay, the work had to be done by men with scythes. With those corrugations and all those deep channels, mechanization of haymaking was impossible.

Very few water-meadows are now maintained in working order, and those are subsidised for the sake of demonstrating what would otherwise be an extinct art. But in recent months, with the entire riparian landscape under water, the old gridiron pattern of baulks and drains has become visible again in many valleys. And, as in the past, the now-unharnessed floods are a paradise for wildfowl.

Starting the day...in slow motion

5th January 1992

I DARE say that many readers, like myself, enjoy spotting anachronisms in films and television programmes. You know the sort of thing – the stage coach draws up at the posting-inn, the passengers all in period costume climb out, and then the illusion of the age of Dickens is wrecked by the sight of an electric light pole in the background. Or Robin Hood is shown hiding behind a rhododendron thicket.

One of the most difficult problems for a producer trying to set a rural scene in the early years of the present century is to get a haymaking or harvesting background right. Time and again I have seen fields decorated with bales of hay or straw. If my memory serves me, the tractor baler did not put in its appearance until the late 1940s or 1950s. Before that, hay-bales or straw-bales were made by hand, at the rick, and tied with hand-woven straw bonds. As a matter of act, only hay or straw to be sold away from the farm was baled; for home consumption it was handled loose, with a prong.

Another pitfall which will beset producers of the future, if it has not already raised its head, will be to create an authentic village background for any period up to the early 1960s. The feature that has transformed the village scene since then is the superabundance of cypress trees. Most of them are Lawson's cypresses – an attractive and useful tree for forming a screen beloved by the new race of village residents, who like to keep their gardens private.

They are slow to start, but once they reach a height of five or six feet they grow several feet a year, making a taller screen than some of their planters bargained for and calling for drastic work with the pruning saw. Still, they are here to stay and, on the whole, they are an asset to the landscape. There can be no doubt, though, that they have completely transformed the rural scene. And any producer who photographs a modern village with a view to using the pictures as a background for a play set in, say, the 1930s will be asking for trouble.

A suburban friend, country-bred, told me that he recently pointed to a bird flying high overhead and remarked to a neighbour,

"Look, there's a jay!"

To his surprise, the neighbour flatly refused to believe him.

"You can't tell what sort of bird it is, flying and at that distance," he declared.

And my friend said he wouldn't be convinced.

It is, of course, quite easy, with experience. The jay, for instance, has a slow, flat flight and a typical crow-like silhouette; no country-man could mistake it. Some birds are more difficult but with practice it is even possible, as a rule, to distinguish between all the thrushes in flight (mistle-thrush, song-thrush, redwing, fieldfare and blackbird), between the numerous finches and even between some of the gulls.

Well, after seventy years of practice I ought to be able to, oughtn't I – but the incident set me thinking about some of the advantages I have gleaned from a lifetime of watching Nature, many of them still ongoing. For instance...I am not one of the natural early-risers. My wife is, but I am not. Get me out of bed at five o'clock in the morning and set me in front of a typewriter, and the paper in it would still be blank at seven. In the evening, however, I can happily tap away on the keys until nigh on midnight. My wife is a dynamo of energy in the mornings but collapses like a punctured tyre in the evenings. She it is who gets up, prepares the breakfast and ruthlessly sweeps the bed-clothes off my still somnolent figure. She complains, with some reason, about the lack of intelligent conversation at the breakfast table.

But half-an-hour later we are taking our morning walk in the woods, and I begin to wake up. I have to, if I am not to miss anything. I have to be alert to spot birds darting across the woodland ride. Sometimes there are a couple of roe deer, briefly visible before fading into the thickets; sometimes a rabbit or, less likely, a hare. At the woodland edge I sweep the panorama of fields with my field-glasses, searching for the pheasants, pigeons, crows, gulls, partridges, lapwings and the odd kestrel, which ought to be there but are sometimes inexplicably absent. I am reminded that I have to keep my eyes skywards as well as groundwards and all around me.

Then there are the sounds. Here my wife has to take over, for my deafness makes it impossible for me to detect the call of the goldcrest or the squeaking of a shrew. But she can hear them, and sometimes she can point them out in time for me to catch a glimpse of them. She is my ears.

We both possess the sense of smell, fortunately undiminished.

"A fox has been across the track here in the night."

I catch up with her and sniff. There is no mistaking the pungent scent of a dog fox. And a little farther on we see where he has been scratching at a mole-hill. We pause for a few minutes' conversation with the woodman, who tells us of a badger he has met strolling along a woodland path, and of where to see crossbills.

So we come to the end of our walk, which has taken us about three-quarters of an hour, with our senses thoroughly awakened and honed for instant use. The mists of sleep have been dispersed, and I am ready to make full use of the day.

The Opportune Owl

16th December 1990

NOW is the season when rats and mice leave their summer homes in fields, hedges, and woodlands and seek warmer winter quarters. It is not often we see mass migrations, like those of the Norwegian lemmings, though once, many years ago I found myself surrounded by scores of voles, trekking along the margin of a hazel wood. More often the only evidence of rodent migration is a noticeable increase in the numbers of rats and mice in a specific locality.

In the days before the coming of combine-harvesters we used to notice the influx in rickyards and farmsteads. A pair of rats taking up residence in a wheat rick would multiply into hundreds before the end of the winter and would devour more grain than they left for the farmer.

Now, of course, although we hear that the old wasteful situation still prevails in Russia, here in England the hungry rodents have to make do with private residences, including mine. Over the past month or two we have had several separate invasions of outhouses and greenhouses by rats and have had the utmost difficulty in persuading them they are not welcome.

So, when at half-past two the other morning our little dog woke me up with frantic barking, I was pleased. "He's barking at an owl," my wife had murmured sleepily, and so I had slipped on my hearing aid. Sure enough, there was an owl in the back garden – and not one but two! In the big beeches a tawny owl was uttering his musical if lugubrious "Hoo – hoo-hoo", as had happened quite recently over the past few months. But tonight there was another, less musical but more persisted voice – a little owl yelping.

I was delighted, for this was the first little owl that had come my way for more than a year. And, of course, any and all owls are very welcome in my garden at present. The most effective of all would naturally be the barn owl, than whom there is no more effective rodent executive, but sadly I have no good news to report on that species. So far I have seen only one Barn Owl in 1990, and several former nesting-sites I used to know have been deserted. Still, the little owl is a useful substitute.

My visitor brought back memories, too, of the 1920s when I first began to take an interest in birds. Little owls were then quite common in our village. We not only heard them at night but frequently saw them, for they were also noisy and conspicuous by day. One reason for this was that they had an ample choice of nesting-sites.

In our village most farm paddocks had their rows of pollarded elms – trees that had had their crowns cut off to encourage them to send out young shoots for growing into fencing-posts in about eight years. The farmers harvested them regularly. And as the harvests came and went, so the trees developed gnarled and knobbled crowns, honeycombed with cavities which provided ideal nesting-sites for certain birds. With starlings they were very popular, but the birds which interested me most were stock doves and little owls.

Both species were far more common than they are now, a decline for which Dutch elm disease must be partly responsible. The only little owl nests I have found in recent years have been on stacks of bales (straw or hay) in open barns.

The story of the little owl could be entitled its 'Rise and Fall' – a saga which lasted less than two hundred years. Owners of rural estates started introducing the species around the middle of last century, but most of the early ventures had a very limited success, and the little owl did not become well established over most of southern England until the 1920s. Almost immediately it was subjected to severe persecution by the gamekeepers employed by those same estate owners – on the assertion that it preyed on young pheasants. Oddly enough, the easing off of the persecution has coincided with a decline in the status of the little owl. Maybe the agricultural use of more effective insecticides – insects, small mammals being the chief food of this owl, may have something to do with it.

The latest census of breeding birds of Britain, undertaken by the British Trust for Ornithology nearly twenty years ago, put the estimated population of little owls at ten thousand pairs, as compared with one hundred thousand for the tawny owl. I would guess there has been a further decline since then.

The barn owl population is estimated at the same level as that of the little owl, and that too has probably declined. If the barn owl were confined to the British Isles it would be teetering on the edge of extinction, but fortunately it has an almost world-wide distribution and in some countries it is flourishing.

A recent letter from Malaysia told me of the barn owl nesting-boxes which are erected in rubber and other commercial plantations, to encourage the birds in their invaluable service in keeping rodents under control. Even more recently a visitor who works in Vancouver airport was telling me of the barn owls which live in the great hangars that house the giant jet planes. Plans to extend one of the buildings have had to be postponed until it is established whether they would interfere with breeding owls.

These pampered owls are luckier than the little owls of the Mediterranean countries, notably Italy, where they are widely used as decoys. There they have become involved in the common human mania for shooting things. Having been captured, a little owl is fitted with a harness and installed on a suitable perch to attract small birds. Inevitably they collect to mob it and are then shot down by the waiting guns. As the victims are, very largely, migrants that nest in northern Europe, we have a vested interest in helping Italian conservationists to outlaw this deplorable practice.

The Spotted Horse goes back a long way

12th January 1992

A SOMERSET reader wrote to tell me: "Recently I saw on a country road a most attractive little spotted horse, drawing a trap. I didn't get a chance to ask the driver about it but understand from neighbours that it is a rare and very old type of animal. Can you tell us anything about it?"

Yes, when I was living in Somerset some fourteen years ago I used to know one of the main breeders of the Somerset Spotted Horses, though I haven't heard from her for the past decade. She then had about fifty mares and six stallions, which must have contributed the greater part of the strength of the type. I was going to write 'breed' but the Spotted Horses seem to have slipped through the net of the breed societies. Pedigree animals are registered with the Welsh Pony and Cob Society, though without reference to their spots.

Some of the horses are the size of large ponies (up to about thirteen hands) but others are miniatures, and their colour is very variable. Some are white with a liberal sprinkling of black spots of varying size, Apalooza style; others are roan or grey, with brown spots; still others have only a thin peppering of spots on the flanks and none on the forequarters.

A three-week-old foal I saw showed the last-named characteristic – a lovely little creature with grey foreparts and a dense cluster of black spots on the rear. But many of the foals are born bay-coloured, gradually changing to white with spots by the end of three years.

The few breeders are convinced that their spotted horses are descended from a prehistoric type of forest horse which once roamed wild in primeval Britain. The spotted colour pattern is typical of forest animals, such as the leopard, the dappling being useful camouflage for an animal living under a tree canopy. There is a theory that the spotted horse was at one time a totem or sacred animal for tribes who lived in Somerset and that associations between this type of horse and the old pagan religion lingered long in these parts, getting spotted horses a bad name with the medieval church. Hence spotted horses are seldom mentioned in medieval documents, though old pictures sometimes depict them.

One breeder told me that it was considered very unlucky to refer to a white horse or pony as anything but 'grey' and even more unlucky to mention the word 'spotted'. The spotted horses were not called 'red-spotted' or 'black-spotted' but 'roans' or 'greys'. She asked an old countryman how, then, he would describe a spotted horse to some-one who had never seen one. He thought he would be happy saying, 'Marked, like yours!' A neat way round the problem. But evidently the word 'spot' had come to mean something bad or taboo. It could well have been that in the distant past the spotted horse had been sacred to a pagan religion and hence has been frowned upon by the Church.

There is also a connection, some way back, with a type known as the Merriott Market Horse, which were also spotted. They were dainty creatures, clean-limbed and with relatively short noses. Their broad foreheads covered a brain-case with a greater capacity than normal for horses of that size, and they were markedly intelligent. They were also docile, friendly and easily managed.

Merriott Horses used to be much in demand for fast transport. From the Crewkerne and Yeovil area they used to race to Weymouth, Bridport, Lyme Regis or some other port with supplies of local produce and return with loads of fish. They also went farther afield to Bristol and Salisbury markets twice a week. And they hauled heavy loads of flax to local rope and sail mills and then transported the ropes and sails to the fleet at Weymouth. One of the versions of the origin of the name 'Halfway Hackney', by which the spotted horses were also known is that when the horses had delivered a load to its destination they were only halfway through their journey. Turning their vehicle around with military precision, they quickly acquired another load and raced back home with it.

The men who drove the horses were sometimes known as 'Merriott tranters', presumably derived from 'transporters'. They maintained that the breed was of very ancient origin and associated it with a stock of horses maintained by the West Saxon king Ina, whose place was situated in the vicinity. And, although many of them were illiterate men, they used to speak of even earlier kings known otherwise only to scholars. Evidently the ancestry of both the spotted horses and their masters is lost in antiquity. There is, by the way, a Spotted Horse Inn at Congresbury, on the edge of the Mendips.

In addition to horses of twelve or thirteen hands there was also a smaller spotted animal of eleven hands or less. It had rather a long body and was known as a 'hand pony'. Its most frequent role was to carry bags of game for sportsmen.

Although the spotted horses are now so scarce in England they still survive and are much in demand by overseas breeders who know about them. An Australian breeder who has fallen in love with them spends his occasional trips to England looking for them and has managed to buy and export several. And an old colleague of mine now resident in Cumberland when last heard of was breeding spotted ponies.

A Day's Beating

16th December 1991

APART from occasional coppers in exchange for odd jobs about my father's farm (and I cannot remember that there were many of those, for in those days one rarely paid for work done by one's family), the first money I ever earned was by going beating on pheasant shoots on the neighbouring estate. It must have been at about this time of the year in the mid-1920s, though perhaps it was in the Christmas school holidays. Anyway, I was, I suppose, eleven or twelve years old. Most of my schoolmates at the village school had already been roped in for duty by the local keepers, and now it was my turn.

We had to report at a locality about two miles from home at eight o'clock in the morning and my mother sent me off with a packed lunch in a school satchel. I wore leather boots and gaiters, for this was before the era of rubber boots. On the way my companions, two boys a year or so older than myself who had been beating before and were therefore, in their opinion, authorities on the matter, regaled me with the benefit of their experience.

"Hang back when they're picking out chaps to go over the fields beyond the woods," they advised. "You gets too much walking over ploughed ground that way. And if you be unlucky enough to get sent on that caper, for goodness' sake don't rush to pick up a hare if one of the guns shoots it. Else you'll have to carry it for miles, and hares gets tarblish heavy when you lugs 'em over ploughed fields."

Fortunately I was given a cushy berth. The head keeper, noticing that I was small and new to the game, sent me with one of his under-keepers and a couple of boys to act as 'stops'.

We retraced our steps for a mile or more along the path we had come and finished up on the edge of a wood. I was given a beat of perhaps a couple of hundred yards to patrol and told to make plenty of noise when I heard the guns coming my way, to keep the pheasants in the wood and prevent them escaping in the wrong direction. Well, that was easy enough, for my beat was in a grass-field. I walked along the hedge conscientiously for a time and met up with the next chap in the line for an occasional chat. The sun came out, and we happened to be on the lee side of the wood, so it was quite pleasant.

By mid-day nothing had happened, so I sat on a log just inside the wood and ate my sandwiches. It wasn't until quite late in the afternoon that the shoot came my way. The beaters came charging and shouting through the wood, working at right angles to my beat, so, taking my cue from the next 'stop', I too shouted and hollered when I heard movements in the wood that might indicate a pheasant. One or two birds flew out high, and I hoped that nobody had noticed them and would blame me for it. On the far side of the wood the guns were blazing away, but they were out of my range of vision. Then all was quiet again.

As dusk closed in the under-keeper came to collect us. We trudged back again to the assembly point, where we lined up and received from the head-keeper our day's pay – half-a-crown. Then back again, the way we had come, and so home. So I had plenty of walking, though from the point of view of the job it was quite unnecessary. From the edge of the wood I made a bee-line across the fields towards home (for I knew every hedge-gap within a couple of miles of our house).

Glancing back, I caught sight of old Henery Frampton, who had a stiff leg and so was always posted as 'stop' somewhere not far from home, still plodding along the edge of the wood and stooping down once or twice to pick up something, and I knew instinctively what it was. He had marked where winged pheasants had dropped during the shoot and was now collecting what he regarded as his 'perks'.

Back at home, I did justice to a cooked meal my mother had waiting for me.

Incidentally, the present generation of youngsters evidently get roped in for the same duties as I did. A thirteen-year-old had his first experience of it recently, so he tells me, though on slightly different terms from those

I obtained. Instead of being paid half-a-crown a day and having to carry my own sandwich lunch, this young man received £5 a day, was taken to a country pub for a hearty cold lunch, and, at the end of the day, was given a pheasant! Well, old Henery Frampton seldom went home from a day's shooting without a pheasant, but he wasn't given it!

Games for a laugh

19th December 1991

CHRISTMAS being a season for memories as well as merriment, I like to dig again into the big box where all the family diaries are kept and jog my mind into remembering events of long-past years. The most assiduous diarist in our family was my mother, who tended to record, however, strictly domestic events. Such as, "Washing day as usual. Not much rain but hardly any drying either." My own efforts are not much more informative. In the late 1920s the entries dealt largely with how much pocket money my father owed me for doing certain jobs at specified rates – a fruitless exercise, incidentally, for this, being the period of the Great Depression, I hardly ever got paid.

However, the feature that struck me most in this year's perusal of the diaries was the remarkable number of Christmas and New Year parties. They seldom started before Christmas because, in the run-up to the festivities everybody was too deeply involved in the preparation of Christmas fatstock. Christmas celebrations in our family began on Christmas Eve, with the hanging-up of pillowcases, and the first party was the family one at home on Christmas Night.

Thereafter the parties came in quick succession. Boxing Day was the occasion of the Grand Village Christmas Party, attended by virtually everyone who was not bedridden. Then we had the Vicar's Christmas Party, the Church Sunday School Christmas Party, the Chapel Sunday

School Christmas Party, the Band of Hope Christmas Party, the Cricket Club Christmas Party, numerous private Christmas parties, and several public Christmas parties in neighbouring villages. Just after the war we also organised a Young Farmers' Club Christmas Party.

Since those days I have attended many Christmas parties of a different type. Office Christmas parties, company Christmas parties, Christmas parties given by sundry organisations, private Christmas parties – and very pleasant most of them have been. However, they nearly all followed the same pattern, which differs in one important respect from the old-time ones. Today we meet and chat, circulating (if the congestion is not too great) with drinks in our hands, but at the old-time parties we played games. Silly games, childish games, but, by heck! we enjoyed them!

At our Village Christmas Party (Held in the old army hut which served our village in lieu of a war memorial) we would start with Musical Knees, Musical Hats or some other version of Musical Chairs and progress to Blowing out the Candle Blindfolded, Passing Balloons (or Matchboxes) without handling them, Avoiding the Hassock, Poor Pussy, Spot Dances, the Okey Okey and other frivolities I have forgotten. After a series of the more exhausting games, such as The Old Stage Coach, we would collapse into whatever chairs we could find to listen to the local comedian give a dialect monologue. Edward Slow's dialect verses were popular items, but the more ambitious lads tried to go one better. Jonas, our star turn, obliged with a string of yarns, culminating with reflection that "Well, now I must be getting along to rack up the hosses." Usually, too, there was a group which sang popular songs – "The Fleet's in Port again", "Let's Have a Tiddly at the Milk Bar" and "We want a Little White Room" are three which I can recall to mind but pop music groups were still a thing of the distant future. We generally finished with community singing of old songs as in the Last Night of the Proms – prompted by reference to the *News Chronicle Song Book*.

Frequently my own role seems to have been that of stooge. I remember that on one occasion I was learning to play the auto-harp and had progressed as far as one tune, which I could perform reasonably well. So they sent me out to the stage to keep the audience quiet for a few minutes while the rest were preparing for the next item. For a few minutes, they said, but the time dragged on. I played my set piece three times, to be urged on to do it yet again by a voice from behind the curtain. In despair I turned to a tune I hadn't properly practised and made a mess of it. I was rescued just before the audience started throwing things at me.

Then there was the time I fancied myself as a conjuror. I started off with the recommended patter and produced the first mystifying trick, but what I didn't know was that my brother had discovered beforehand how each one worked and had primed some of his pals.

"That's simple," they shouted out, "We could do that!"

"All right, come and do it then," I challenged, falling for the trap. And they came out and did just that. Being slow on the uptake, I repeated this four or five times before I realised what was happening. Needless to say, the audience loved it. I have often thought since that I missed a golden opportunity for working out a television act like Tommy Cooper's many years before he came on to the stage.

One year I wrote a Christmas play for children, and we performed it at the Christmas party. It was a pantomime but it served the same purpose. Its title, *The Kidnapping of Father Christmas*. I think, it went down all right. It might have been better with a more efficient producer (who happened to be me), but I fear I enjoyed the rehearsals too much. They were hilarious.

Such are some of my Christmas party memories. To savour them properly you would have to imagine a dusty, overcrowded old army hut, lit by swinging oil-lamps and heated by a slow-combustion, coal-burning stove, with the snow drifting down outside and threatening to cut the village off from 'civilisation' for the next week and nobody caring one bit!.

Also by Ralph Whitlock and published by Ex Libris Press:

THE SECRET LANE

Set in the nineteen-thirties, this is the haunting story of an enchanted summer in an English countryside that has vanished forever.

Steve Maidment is nineteen-years-old, works on his father's farm and is walking out with a girl from the village. Together they seek to unravel the Secret of the Lane, an enigma which has baffled his old Uncle Walter for many years.

The annual cycle of farm and village activities is hardly upset when a party arrives to conduct an archaeological dig at one of the ancient burial mounds nearby, but Steve's attraction to a beautiful American girl helper steers his life far from its predictable course.

Various secrets are revealed in the course of the story, but the real Secret of the Lane is not discovered until the closing pages, after many eventful episodes which involve a host of country characters and seasonal pursuits.

Set in the author's fictional village of Nadderbourne, the rolling downland landscape of South Wiltshire is the recognisable setting for this story. The author writes with a deep knowledge and appreciation of the natural world around him – the story contains much that is evocative of the birds and flowers and changing seasons.

The Secret Lane is Ralph Whitlock's first novel; Ex Libris Press is proud to be its publisher.

159 pages;
double page map *Price £4.95*